T0208982

*The* Book *of* Mystical Chapters

# THE BOOK OF MYSTICAL CHAPTERS

MEDITATIONS
ON THE
SOUL'S ASCENT,
FROM THE
DESERT FATHERS
AND OTHER EARLY
CHRISTIAN
CONTEMPLATIVES

*Translated and introduced by*
*John Anthony McGuckin*

SHAMBHALA
*Boston & London*
2003

SHAMBHALA PUBLICATIONS, INC.

HORTICULTURAL HALL

300 MASSACHUSETTS AVENUE

BOSTON, MASSACHUSETTS 02115

*www.shambhala.com*

Printed in the United States of America

♾ This edition is printed on acid-free paper that meets the
American National Standards Institute z39.48 Standard.
♻ Shambhala Publications makes every effort to
print on recycled paper. For more information
please visit www.shambhala.com.
Distributed in the United States by Random House, Inc.,
and in Canada by Random House of Canada Ltd

The Library of Congress catalogues the hardcover
edition of this book as follows:
The book of mystical chapters: meditations on the
soul's ascent, from the desert fathers and other early
Christian contemplatives / translated and introduced by
John Anthony McGuckin.
p. cm.
Includes bibliographical references (p. ).
ISBN 978-1-57062-900-6
ISBN 978-1-59030-007-7 (paperback)
1. Desert Fathers—Quotations. 2. Spiritual life—
Christianity—Quotations, maxims, etc.
I. McGuckin, John Anthony.
BR63 .B57 2002
248.4'811—dc21
2001057553

# CONTENTS

*The* Book *of* Mystical Chapters

# INTRODUCTION

## *A Guide to the Mystical Path*

The early Christian monks left behind them a vast body of esoteric literature that is profound in the range and quality of the mystical teaching it offers, though by and large it is little known to the contemporary world. Because of their lifestyle of radical simplicity and withdrawal, the monks were able to devote much time to scrutinizing the stages and forms of the inner life of the human spirit. In a sense they were professionals of the mapping of the movements of the interior soul and composed their doctrine specifically for the instruction of their younger disciples. Younger monks and sometimes nuns would frequently travel the monastic communities of the east Roman world seeking out experienced psychic guides (though nuns were usually sedentary in communities lodged in more secure places), and soon the finest of these spiritual masters became internationally known, attracting disciples from all over the Christian territories. The sayings of the wise teachers were soon put into writing—sometimes by the sages themselves in their own lifetime, and sometimes they were gathered together from oral history as a posthumous memorial of their doctrine.

This book is a portable collection of that Christian monastic wisdom, a very small edition of the vast amount of teachings that exist and are still used in the monasteries of the Eastern Christian world to this day. It has been arranged, in the manner of an ancient manual of instruction, in three ascending books: Praktikos, Theoretikos, and Gnostikos. The "sentences" (which in ancient Greek meant a unit of thought, or paragraph) have been edited, again in the ancient manner, in the form of three "centuries," or groups of one hundred aphorisms. Each single sentence is meant to be taken as a day's reflection. It was first supposed to be learned by heart, at the beginning of the day, and then repeated as the daily text in every spare moment of quiet. Such moments of *hesychia* (quietness of soul) were structured by the early monks around the simple repetitive tasks that made up daily life in remote deserts. The regular monotony of basket weaving (a favored monastic employment) was interspersed with the repetition of prayers and the musing on the "sentence" of the day. Today life is busier and more demanding, but even the busiest of us have moments of *hesychia*, in those times spent waiting for buses or trains to arrive or depart, or when we are driving or walking or simply sitting idly for a moment. Such times are ideally suited for the recitation of the sentence and its dialectic—teasing out the implications of what such an aphorism could mean: how have we already experienced it; how could it illuminate a truth about our own heart or the troubles of our friends' hearts or the secret ways that God wishes to develop our seeking soul?

The book, in short, is not meant for a rapid half-hour read-through from cover to cover in one sitting. Such is the temptation for a world gone mad for speed and instant comprehension. It would be better to employ this book as a Frisbee than to use it in that way. Some things, like seeds and plants (and psychic insight), need a slower pace of nurturing and unfolding. The book will be, I hope, an interesting historical example of the esoteric spiritual teachings of the early Christians, who could once boast many masters of the mystical life. But more than this, it is offered as a practical "manual of assistance" for those who wish to climb the higher paths of mystical knowledge in the Christian tradition and—in an age when living spiritual masters are difficult to come by—need experienced guides to orient them.

## MONASTIC SEEKERS IN THE ANCIENT CHURCH

The early Christian monks formed an international society that flourished in all the Greek territories of the late Roman Empire, as well as in Syria and Persia, in Egypt gathered around the Nile, and as far into Africa as Nubia (modern Sudan) and the highlands of Ethiopia. They inhabited the rocky and desert terrain of Sinai, Palestine, Arabia, and Turkey (ancient Cappadocia); and in the great capital of the late Roman Empire, Constantinople, they became almost a civil service, so great were their numbers, with many dedicated scholars and aristocrats among them. After the fifth century, monasticism became popular in the West too, where Gaul (ancient France) and Italy became centers of activity. Soon, over the whole early-Christian world, which was drawn like a circle around the Mediterranean basin, Christian monks could be found living in solitary isolation near villages, in small communes of hermits gathered together in remote valleys, or in small houses, usually of a few dozen living the communal life together. These three forms of monastic lifestyle in the early church had become standard by the fourth century of the common era, and after Constantine had begun the transformation of the Roman state into the Christian empire of Byzantium, the monastic movement flourished for more than a thousand years with the patronage of Christian emperors. In centers such as Athos on the Acte Peninsula, near Halkidiki, in Greece, the Pechersky Lavra (Monastery of the Caves) in Kiev, or the wooded mountain monasteries of Transylvania, this is a way of life that has continued with an ancient vigor into the modern era.

## THE FORMS OF MONASTIC LITERATURE

Over the course of this long history, a massive body of esoteric doctrine was accumulated and distilled by the monks for their own guidance in traveling the paths of the mystical life. The complete dedication of their lives to the search for God, in a radically simplified and poor lifestyle of disciplined work, celibate chastity, and study of the sacred writings of the prophets and saints who had preceded

them, made for a radical focus in their lives that is hard
to imagine in the random complexities and relativities that
form the context of modern Western societies. The literature, from the early third century, attained considerable
sophistication. Teachers such as Origen of Alexandria, one
of the most erudite Platonist philosophers of his age, created an extensive and elegant system for scriptural exegesis
and the methods needed for purifying the soul and assist-
ing its illumination and ascent. All later efforts to advance
a distinctively Christian "spiritual theology" were based,
to a large degree, on his work. Evagrios of Pontus, another
major intellectual of the early Christian period, was one
of the more successful in combining the high intellective
tradition of Origen with the day-to-day needs of communities of ascetics seeking advanced guidance in spiritual
psychology.

As Christianity developed and spread as a state religion,
it turned its thoughts more and more to the rationalistic
defense of its theology. This tendency was accelerated as
large sections of the international Christian movement entered into disputes over doctrinal issues and the Roman
emperors, in response, gave to the theological decisions of
the bishops (meeting for conciliar debates) the force of
Roman law. The monastic texts, by contrast, were largely
uninterested in controversial argument. It was a literature
dedicated to the secrets of the inner life, a quest for the
paths of peacefulness, mercy, and purity of prayer. Over
long centuries the rationalistic spirit of Christian argu-
mentation has barely subsided. Many generations have
come and gone, producing the controversial literature of

their own ages. The Western movement later known as the Reformation preached a gospel of free grace apprehended by faith alone; the monastic attempt to work out salvation partly through ascetic efforts was anathema to it. The resulting collapse of the monastic tradition in large parts of Europe further contributed to the formalistic rationalizing of the spirit of Western Christianity and impoverished its tradition of mystical teaching. In the Eastern Christian world, no reformation was ever experienced. Its philosophical and cultural unity, with a few short-lived exceptions, ran on in a deep organic relation with the principles of Hellenistic culture that had been laid down in antiquity. The Byzantines regarded their religious and cultural system as Hellenism baptized into the Gospel; and certainly that perennial Roman political passion for cultural unity was maintained, yet with a corresponding celebration of individual freedom. It was this flexible mix that avoided the kind of centralist control observable in the Western church that then led inevitably to large-scale nationalist revolts in the late Middle Ages.

The rise of Islam in the original heartlands of the Eastern church curtailed the freedoms of Christians for centuries but led to a certain blessed obscuring of the life of monasteries that survived—and survive they did, in large numbers. The life of these Eastern Orthodox monasteries follows, often unchanged, the patterns of the primitive communities, and in them the spiritual texts of the esoteric tradition have been carefully preserved, copied, and transmitted as the basic training of new generations of spiritual seekers, a common culture that still unites the Christian East from Syria to Romania and from Ethiopia to Russia.

## THE THREEFOLD ASCENT: PRAXIS, THEORIA, AND GNOSIS

The earliest writers tended to divide their spiritual teachings into three basic categories, suitable for the stages of first searchers, young monks of several years' standing, and finally, the more advanced. The instructions were usually arranged as short paragraphs, meant to be learned by heart and meditated on over and over again for a day or even a week until the paragraph had broken like a fruit on the tongue of the monk and revealed its inner flavor to the searching mind. The same practice was adopted in regard to phrases from the Scriptures, especially the Psalms. Biblical texts are frequently referred to in the monastic writings, and I have given note references that provide the chapter and verse. Those who look them up should know that the monks always quoted the Greek Septuagint version of the Bible, which is often different from the current translations of the Scriptures in common use today, both in text and in numbering system (Psalms are usually one number out of alignment). In addition, the monks often alluded to texts rather than giving a precise rendering of them, a sign that they were quoting from memory, as copies of the sacred writings in antiquity were not usually found in every private cell, only in the main church building.

The short paragraphs meant for memorization were

called *kephalaia* in the Greek, which means "text headings," or "chapters." The collections of these monastic manuals of instruction, therefore, were often called Books of Chapters. The first stage of teachings was called Praktikos. This was like a stage of "exercises," or basic matters of technique and preparation in the life of prayer and mystical searching. It was predominantly concerned with the need for disciplined attention and the skills required to scrutinize the often complex paths that made up the psyche of the searcher. It was a firm belief of the monks, based upon the Christian idea that the soul was made after the image and likeness of God, that a mastery of the knowledge of the inner self was necessary before one could presume to discern the more mysterious workings of the divine Spirit in a human life. The contemporary word *psychology* (and perhaps even the focused modern interest in psychology as a quest for the authentic self) derives from the Christian interest in mapping out the inner life of the monk as a first stage in mystical journeying. The word is taken from the Greek and signifies "the study of the inner soul." The impressive twentieth-century advances in psychological understanding have rendered obsolete some of the ancient psychological teaching (particularly its ready ascription of passionate desires to demonic influence), but they have not superseded its central tradition of wisdom. This is especially true in regard to what it was trying to say about spiritual subjectivity, or the unmasking of the multiple versions of the false self we often construct, or the quest for personal psychic calm, integrity, and stability. Moreover, although "psychologia" was of fundamental importance for the early Christians, it was only the first stage in a threefold path of increasingly transcendent journeying.

The second stage of advancement, after Praktikos, was designated Theoretikos. This was a technical term for "seeing" and referred to the spiritual state when the basics of moral and ascetic discipline could be taken for granted (for the celibate ascetics of the desert, this was a considerable physical undertaking involving long vigils, fasts, and the observance of personal chastity and compassion for others). Once the lessons of Praktikos had been absorbed, the spiritual quester moved on to seek guidance in resolving the difficulties of the inner life. The second stage focuses on what were the recurrent problems that stopped a spiritual person from progressing. The level of Theoretikos is like that developmental stage in a musician's career when the elementary exercises have been completed but the player wishes to break through the barrier of the limitation of his or her present technique to reach a stage of virtuosic ability. What is it that prevents different individuals from advancing beyond their prejudices, and repressions, so as to become increasingly illuminated? Theoria probes this issue from a variety of angles.

The third stage of the monastic instructions was reserved for more experienced monks and was often the subject of long discussions from which junior monks would be excluded. This stage was called Gnostikos. It is a word that means the state of knowing, or understanding. In Christian circles, from the late third century onward, when the writings of the earlier gnostic movement had largely been sidelined by the main tradition's bishops and theologians, it was used as a technical term in monastic literature to connote esoteric speculation and reflections on the higher mysteries. Many of these later Christian "gnostic treatises" also fell under the disapproval of the bishops and were suppressed, or even destroyed. Some of the gnostic chapters survived, however, as the more advanced monks kept the tradition of spiritual wisdom alive, despite all opponents—those outside the church and even those within it—who have often tried to stifle the inner currents of Christian mysticism because of their unease with a fiercely personal wisdom tradition that was not always easy to control or define. The books of gnostic chapters are often enigmatic and difficult to interpret. Unlike the other two types of book, the practical and the theoretical chapters, they were not meant to be a teaching tool for those who had not yet experienced such things. The gnostic chapters, by contrast, were meant to be a signal to those who had already experienced some of these things that others were around them who had also experienced the moving of the divine Spirit within and who were ready to communicate on an equal level about the higher mysteries.

## THE DESERT MOTHERS

Unlike the second millennium of Christianity, during which the voice of female teachers has risen with new vigor and insight, the Christian women of the first thousand years were not generally allowed much access to the expensive literary education that was the fundamental preparation of all the rhetoricians and writers of antiquity.

Accordingly, though their voices were certainly present and vital in the affairs of the church, and in the currents of mystical life, they are not well represented in the textual monastic tradition. Names of great female monastics and visionaries have been preserved: Syncletica, Sarra, Proba, Macrina, Melania, Prisca, Perpetua, and many others. But such women, who stood at the heart of female ascetic communities as directing "ammas" (that is, mothers, or spiritual elders), did not typically leave behind rhetorical treatises as did the men, who were in many cases also ordained priests and bishops as well as monks. Perhaps another volume from the second millennium of mystical Christianity would serve better to honor the female teaching tradition. In this present book, Amma Syncletica and Amma Sarra alone represent the ancient female elders.

## A LITTLE *PHILOKALIA*

In the eighteenth century, monks of Mount Athos (the still-surviving Byzantine monastic colony on the Acte Peninsula in Greece) collated many of the major writings of the great monastic corpus into a multivolume collection that they entitled *Philokalia* (The Lover of Beautiful Things). This continues to be one of the chief inspirational collections for all Eastern Orthodox monasteries to the present time. Our present book, which takes many of its source texts from that old Greek collection, is itself a little *Philokalia*. It represents the greatest of the esoteric Christian sages from the Greek Byzantine, Libyan, Egyptian, Palestinian, Syrian, and Persian traditions, writing in the first millennium.

Most of the writers present here wrote in Greek. Several Coptic and Syrian teachers have also been preserved in their own tongues as well as in Greek and Latin translations from ancient times. The translations from Greek and Latin are my own. The original Syriac versions of writers such as John of Dalyutha, Sahdona the Syrian, and Narsai of Edessa have recently been published. In these cases, I have translated from the critical French editions of these manuscripts. I hope, by presenting the teachings of all these sages in an accessible form, that they will continue their task of instructing and challenging, in a certain transcendence of time that so many of them aspired to. I hope that they prove to be illuminating, in every sense.

JOHN A. McGUCKIN
*Feast of the Transfiguration of*
*Jesus on the Mountain*
August 6, 2001

# BOOK ONE

## *Praktikos*
### A Century of
### Practical Chapters

## 1

Snow can never emit flame.
Water can never issue fire.
A thorn bush can never produce a fig.
Just so, your heart can never be free
from oppressive thoughts, words, and actions
until it has purified itself internally.
Be eager to walk this path.
Watch your heart always.
Constantly say the prayer
"Lord Jesus Christ, have mercy on me."
Be humble.
Set your soul in quietness.

—*Hesychios*

## 2

One of the monks asked the great teacher
Abba Nistero:
"What should I do for the best in life?"
And the abba answered:
"All works are not equal.
The scripture says that Abraham was hospitable,
and God was with him;
it says that Elias loved quiet,

and God was with him;
it says that David was humble,
and God was with him.
So, whatever path you find your soul longs after
in the quest for God,
do that, and always watch over your heart's integrity."

—*Sayings of the Elders*


## 3

Abba Antony said:
Whoever sits in solitude and is quiet
has escaped from three wars:
those of hearing, speaking, and seeing.
Then there is only one war left in which to fight,
and that is the battle for your own heart.

—*Sayings of the Elders*


## 4

Amma Sarra said:
If I prayed to God
that all men should approve of my conduct,
I should find myself endlessly penitent

before each man's door.
I shall not ask this;
I shall pray instead
that my heart might be pure toward all.

—*Apophthegmata Patrum*

# 5

Keep a careful watch on yourself.
Do not allow yourself to be swept away
by external obsessions.
The tumultuous movements of the soul,
in particular,
can be rendered quiet by stillness.
But if you keep encouraging and stimulating them,
they will start to terrorize you
and can disorder your whole life.
Once they are in control, it is as hard to heal them
as it is to soothe a sore that we can't stop scratching.

—*Abba Philemon*

# 6

Set your mind on following the path of saints.
Prefer a simple style of life.

Wear unremarkable clothes.
Eat simple food.
Behave in an unaffected manner.
Don't strut around as if you were important.
Speak from your heart.

—*Abba Philemon*


# 7

After our baptism, an even greater baptism—
if I may make so bold as to put it that way—
is the baptism provided by our tears.
Our first baptism cleansed all our former sins. . . .
The baptism of our tears cleanses us anew
by the gift of compassion
God gives to the human race.

—*John Klimakos*


# 8

Our Lord told us to pray in secret—
that means in your heart—
MATT. 6:6  and he instructed us to "shut the door."
What is this door he says we must shut,

if not the mouth?
For we are the temple in which Christ dwells,
for as the Apostle said:
"You are the temple of the Lord."  1 COR. 3:16
And the Lord enters into your inner self,
into this house,
to cleanse it from everything that is unclean,
but only while the door—that is, your mouth—
is closed shut.

—*Aphrahat the Persian*

# 9

From the moment you start praying,
raise your heart upward
and turn your eyes downward.
Come to focus in your innermost self
and there pray in secret to your heavenly Father.

—*Aphrahat the Persian*

# 10

Before you pray,
first forgive all those who have offended you,

then pray.
Only then will your prayer rise up
into the presence of God.
If you do not forgive,
it will simply remain on the earth.

*—Aphrahat the Persian*

# 11

When you pray, be mindful
that you are in the presence of God,
offering a priestly sacrifice.
Would it not be a shameful thing
to offer a sacrifice that was blemished?
So, as you pray to be forgiven,
first forgive those who have offended you.
Bring them to mind and pardon them,
and then you yourself will also know
God's forgiveness.

*—Aphrahat the Persian*

# 12

A young calf starts to wander after fresh grazing
and eventually finds itself stranded

among frightful chasms.
So it is with the soul,
for thoughts gradually lead it astray.

*—Mark the Ascetic*

# 13

If we purify ourselves of wickedness,
then we will come to see invisible realities.
But there is no point, while we are still blind,
in asking why it is we cannot see the light,
no point in stuffing our ears
and then asking why it is we cannot hear anything.

*—John of Apamea*

# 14

A disciple should always carry
the memory of God within.
For it is written:
You shall love the Lord your God
with all your heart.                    DEUT. 6:5
You should not only love the Lord
when entering into the place of prayer

but should also remember him with deep desire
when you walk or speak to others
or take your meals.
For scripture says: Where your heart is,

MATT. 6:21 there also is your treasure;
and surely, wherever a person's heart is given,
wherever their deepest desire draws them,
this is indeed their god.
If a disciple's heart always longs for God,
then God will surely be the Lord of the heart.

*—Makarios the Great*

## 15

If your mind can pray without distraction,
your heart will soon be softened.
And, as it says in scripture:
"God will never scorn a heart

Ps. 51:17 that is humbled and distressed."

*—Mark the Ascetic*

## 16

If we want to set our lives right and find peace,
it is not the tolerant attitude of others

that will do it for us.
It will come about, rather, by our learning
how to show compassion to them.
If we try to avoid this hard struggle of compassion,
by preferring a withdrawn and solitary life,
we will simply drag our unhealed obsessions
into solitude with us.
We might well have hidden them.
We certainly will not have eliminated them.
If we do not seek liberation from our obsessions,
then becoming more withdrawn and less social
may even make us more blind to them,
since it can mask them.

—*John Cassian*

## 17

If we take Saint Paul literally,
we are not allowed to cling to our anger
even for a day.                                        EPH. 4:26
I would like to make a comment, however,
that many people are so embittered and furious
when they are in a state of anger
that they not only cling to their anger for a day
but drag it out for weeks.
I am at a loss for words to explain

those who do not even vent their anger in speech
but erect a barrier of sullen silence around them
and distill the bitter poison of their hearts
until it finally destroys them.
They could not have understood
how important it is to avoid anger,
not merely externally, but even in our thoughts,
because it darkens our intellect with bitterness
and cuts it off from the radiance
of spiritual understanding and discernment
by depriving it of the indwelling of the Holy Spirit.

—*John Cassian*

## 18

Luke
23:40–43 The thief on the cross certainly did not receive
the Kingdom of Heaven as a reward for his virtues
but as a grace and mercy from God.
He can serve as an authentic witness
that our salvation is given to us
only by God's mercy and grace.
All the holy masters knew this
and unanimously taught that perfection in holiness
can be achieved only through humility.

—*John Cassian*

# 19

If you are tired and worn out
by your labors for your Lord,
place your head upon his knee and rest awhile.
Recline upon his breast,                    JOHN 13:23
breathe in the fragrant spirit of life,
and allow life to permeate your being.
Rest upon him, for he is a table of refreshment        Ps. 23:5
that will serve you the food of the divine Father.

—*John of Dalyutha*

# 20

A man may want to protect his household valuables
from the predations of thieves,
but he will be frustrated in his efforts
if his cries are drowned out
by the noise of the crowds outside.
So it is with the soul in the body, for its powers too
are often drowned out by bad things.
The soul is in the body almost as if it were not there.
It abides there often without manifesting its powers.
God did not ordain
that the soul should be in the body
and yet still be able to move

without relation to the body's characteristics.
As long as the soul is in the body,
its own senses are inoperative.
As soon as it separates from the body,
it can move in and of itself.
And this separation need not be understood
only as if it were a question
of the soul's leaving the body,
for it can also be considered as the separation
of the psychic awareness from the body.
Though the soul may still be in the body,
it surely finds itself outside the body.
While the body still moves in the world,
the psychic consciousness transcends the world.
This is what the Savior meant when he said:

JOHN 15:19 "But you are not of this world."

—*John of Apamea*

## 21

A monk once said to Abba Philemon:
"I am very conscious of how my mind
constantly wanders all over the place,
drifting after things that are not good for it.
What can I do, father, to be delivered?"
And he hesitated for a little while and then replied:

"This is a remnant of the obsessions
your external life inflicts on you.
It still troubles you because you have not yet
reached the heights of perfect longing for God.
The longing for the experience of God
has not yet fallen on you like fire."

—*Abba Philemon*

## 22

When the soul has been purified
by keeping the commandments,
the spiritual intellect[1] can be ordered and stabilized;
only then can it reach that state
it needs to attain for prayer.

—*Evagrios of Pontus*

## 23

Try to make your spiritual intellect deaf and dumb
during the time of prayer,
for then you will really be able to pray.

—*Evagrios of Pontus*

## 24

If you store up grievances
and nurse old animosities inside yourself,
and then try to pray,
you will be like someone going to the well for water
with a bucket that is full of holes.

—*Evagrios of Pontus*

## 25

Always be on your guard against your anger,
and then you will not be carried away
by other violent desires.
Anger gives fuel to all sorts of other passions
and always clouds the spiritual eye,
disrupting the state of pure prayer.

—*Evagrios of Pontus*

## 26

Sometimes it happens that when you start to pray,
you find you can pray well.
At other times,
even when you have expended great effort,

you may find your efforts frustrated.
This experience is to make you learn
that you must exert yourself constantly,
for having once gained the gift of prayer,
you must be careful to keep it safe.

*—Evagrios of Pontus*

## 27

Do not pray for your heart's desires,
for they may not entirely harmonize
with God's purposes.
Pray instead as you have been taught:
"May your will be done in me."          Luke 22:42
Pray to God this way about everything,
that his will might be accomplished in you,
for he only desires what is good and useful
for your life,
whereas you do not always request this.

*—Evagrios of Pontus*

## 28

I have often prayed and asked God
for what seemed good in my own estimation.

Like a fool, I kept on at God to grant me this;
I would not leave it to him
to arrange as he knows best for me.
Then, having obtained the thing
I had prayed for so stubbornly,
I have often been sorry
that I did not leave it to the will of God,
for the reality often turned out very different
from the way I had imagined.

—*Evagrios of Pontus*


## 29

Whether you pray alone
or in the company of others,
try never to pray simply as a matter of routine
but always with conscious awareness
of what you are doing.

—*Evagrios of Pontus*


## 30

When you pray,
keep a careful watch on your faculty of memory

so that it does not distract you
with images of your past
but instead reminds you
in whose presence you stand,
for it is in the nature of our spiritual intellect
that it can get carried away by memories
during the time of prayer.

—*Evagrios of Pontus*


# 31

The dark powers are sick with envy against us
when we pray,
and they will use every conceivable trick
to frustrate us spiritually.
They endlessly stir up our inner memories
to distract us into thoughts
and will try to stir our flesh to all kinds of desires,
for in this way
they think they can hinder the soul's glorious ascent
and its journey to God.

—*Evagrios of Pontus*


# 32

If you want to experience true prayer,
then seek to control your anger and your desires.

But more than this,
you must also strive to liberate yourself
from every material thought.

—*Evagrios of Pontus*

## 33

When your spiritual intellect longs for God so deeply
that little by little it loses interest in material things
and turns away from all thoughts
rooted in sensory perception,
or those that rise from our temperament
or our memories,
and at the same time becomes more and more
filled with a sense of reverence and joy,
then know that you have drawn near
to the threshold of prayer.

—*Evagrios of Pontus*

## 34

Someone who is tied up cannot run.
Just so, the spiritual intellect
that is still a slave to its obsessive desires

can never see the domain of spiritual prayer,
because it is dragged all over the place
by compulsive ideations[2]
and cannot achieve
the necessary intellectual stillness.

—*Evagrios of Pontus*

## 35

Know this:
that the holy angels encourage us to pray,
and when we do pray,
they stand beside us with great joy,
praying for us.
But if we grow careless
and admit wicked thoughts,
we greatly vex the angels,
for there they are struggling hard on our behalf,
and we cannot even be bothered
to pray to God for our own benefit
but have scorned their assistance
and dishonored their master and their God.

—*Evagrios of Pontus*

## 36

Prepare yourself like a professional wrestler.
Even if you see a sudden apparition,
do not be alarmed . . .
but be careful in case evil spirits
try to deceive you with visions.
If this happens, be very attentive;
turn immediately to prayer
and ask God to enlighten you himself
whether this vision is from him
and, if it is not,
to drive the illusion away from you at once.
Be of good courage,
for if you make your prayer to God with burning zeal,
these dogs of wicked spirits will trouble you no longer
but will immediately be whipped away
by the unseen power of the Lord.

—*Evagrios of Pontus*


## 37

As bread is food for the body
and holiness is food for the soul,
so spiritual prayer is food for the interior mind.

—*Evagrios of Pontus*

# 38

Do not run away from poverty or sorrows;
such things lift our prayer to heaven.

*—Evagrios of Pontus*

# 39

It is very dangerous to reach out boldly,
without any sense of shame,
for the knowledge of divine things
or to set off on a life dedicated to immaterial prayer
when we are still caught fast
in the nets of sinfulness and anger.
We would deserve the Apostle's rebuke
when he tells us that our soul, when it prays,
ought to wear a veil over its head
on account of the angels who are present.          1 Cor. 11:5
That is, we must first clothe our soul
in due reverence and humility.

*—Evagrios of Pontus*

# 40

If your eyes are hurting you,
it will certainly not help to stand gazing

into the glare of the noonday sun.
In the same way,
the fearful practice of transcendent prayer—
something that can be accomplished
JOHN 4:23   only "in spirit and in truth"—
will be of no use whatsoever
to a spiritual intellect that is still impassioned
and unclean.
What is more:
if such a spirit should try to practice this prayer,
it may even rouse the anger of God
against its presumption.

*—Evagrios of Pontus*

## 41

God is in want of nothing
and shows no particular favoritism,
but he certainly did not want to receive that man
who came to him with a sacrificial gift
until he had first been reconciled with his neighbor
MATT. 5:23   who had a grievance against him.
So think, and discern carefully
how you ought to offer spiritual incense to God

on the altar of your spirit,
so that it will indeed be an acceptable gift.

—*Evagrios of Pontus*

## 42

If you seek after prayer with concentration,
then you will surely find prayer.
Nothing is more essential to prayer
than concentration.
Do all that you can to acquire it.

—*Evagrios of Pontus*

## 43

If you find your intellect wanders,
then reading, nighttime vigils, and prayer
will bring it to stillness.
Fasting, hard manual work, and quiet solitude
calm the fires of desire.
To calm your restlessness,
sit and recite the book of psalms
and have pity and compassion

for all those around you.
If you do excessive and inappropriate exercises,
it will all come to grief very quickly,
and this will cause you more harm than good.

*—Evagrios of Pontus*

## 44

A tree will never blossom without water.
Without mystical knowledge
the heart will never rise on high.

*—Evagrios of Pontus*

## 45

How lovely is prayer,
and how radiant are its works.
Prayer is acceptable to God
when it goes with good deeds,
and it is heard when it rises
out of a spirit of forgiveness.
Prayer is always answered
when it is pure and sincere.

Prayer is powerful
when it is suffused with God's vigor.

—*Aphrahat the Persian*

# 46

It was a saying of Amma Syncletica's
that just as bitter medicine purged poison,
so prayer and fasting purged our evil thoughts.

—*Apophthegmata Patrum*

# 47

Do not be surprised
if you fall back into the old ways every day.
Do not be disheartened
but resolve to do something positive,
and without question,
that angel who stands guard over you
will honor your perseverance.

—*John Klimakos*

## 48

If we dwell on hurts that others have given us,
we will be like those bizarre interpreters of scripture
who read the spiritual text in any way that suits them.
Put this attitude to shame within you
by reciting the Jesus Prayer:
"Lord Jesus Christ, have mercy on us."

*—John Klimakos*

## 49

All people are able to pray in a congregation.
Many others find it much better
to pray with a single like-minded companion.
Solitary prayer is suitable for very few indeed.

*—John Klimakos*

## 50

A furnace puts gold to the test.
The assiduous practice of prayer
tests a disciple's zeal and love for God.

*—John Klimakos*

# 51

The angel Lucifer fell from heaven
solely on account of one passion—his pride.
It makes me wonder whether it is possible
to rise up to heaven
solely on the strength of humility.

—*John Klimakos*

# 52

When a ray of sunlight enters the house
through a crack,
it lights up everything inside
and even shows up the finest dust in its beam.
So it is with the fear of the Lord,
when it enters a human heart,
it reveals all the fallibility still lurking there.

—*John Klimakos*

# 53

If you cannot avoid grave lapses,
because of bodily weakness,
you must take the road of humility

and all its qualities,
for there is no other road
that will lead you back to salvation.

—*John Klimakos*

## 54

Stillness of spirit is an endless worship of God
and a standing in the very Presence.
Let the memory of the name of Jesus
be present in every breath you take,
and then you will know the value of stillness.

—*John Klimakos*

## 55

If you keep a vigil,
devote the main part of the night to prayer
and only a little part to the recitation of the Psalter.

—*John Klimakos*

## 56

When you go out after prayer,
keep your tongue under restraint,

for it is well capable of dissipating,
in a very short time,
what you labored to gather together.

—*John Klimakos*

# 57

When you are ready to stand
in the presence of the Lord,
let your soul wear a garment woven throughout
from the cloth of our forgiveness of others.
Otherwise your prayer will be
of no value whatsoever.

—*John Klimakos*

# 58

Let all your prayer be completely simple.
Both the tax collector and the prodigal son
were reconciled to God by one simple phrase—
one said: God, have mercy on me, a sinner,     Luke 18:9–14
and the other: Father, I have sinned against you.     Luke 15:11–32

—*John Klimakos*

## 59

If, in the course of your prayers,
you feel a special joy
or are moved in the heart by something,
then stay with it for a while.
It is a sign that your guardian angel has come
and begun to pray with you.

*—John Klimakos*

## 60

If you are serious about the life of prayer,
take care to be very merciful, for in this way
MARK 10:30    "you shall receive a hundredfold reward"
and even greater things in the future age.

*—John Klimakos*

## 61

Abba Agathon said:
In my opinion, no other labor is as difficult
as prayer to God.
Every time a person wants to pray,
our spiritual enemies want to come and disrupt it,

for they know that it is only by deflecting
humans from prayer
that they can do them any harm.
Whatever good work a person undertakes
will produce success, if it is done with perseverance,
but the labor of prayer
is a warfare that will endure
until our very last breath.

*—Apophthegmata Patrum*

## 62

Abba Agathon said:
I have never allowed myself to go to bed
while I still felt resentment against a person,
And, as far as I was able,
I never allowed anyone else to go to bed either,
as long as they still felt resentment against me.

*—Apophthegmata Patrum*

## 63

Abba Poemen often used to say that
malice could never overcome malice.

So if anyone acts maliciously toward you,
do good to them in return;
for in this way you will extinguish malice
by kindness.

—*Sayings of the Elders*

# 64

A monk came to Abba Sisoes and said:
"What should I do, Abba,
for I have fallen from grace?"
And he replied, "Get up again."
The monk came back shortly after and said:
"What shall I do now, for I have fallen again?"
And the old man said to him,
"Just get up again.
Never cease getting back up again!"

—*Sayings of the Elders*

# 65

One of the monks asked an elder
for advice on the spiritual life,
and he said: "Do battle vigorously!"

But the monk replied:
"But my thoughts oppress me constantly."
And the old man said to him:
"Scripture says,
'Call on me in the day of your distress,
and I will deliver you,
and then you will bless my name.'
So it is clear:
Call upon God to deliver you
from the mind's oppression."

Ps. 49:15<br>LXX

*—Sayings of the Egyptian Fathers*

## 66

Make it your study
to acquire a long perspective
on your many thoughts.

*—Sayings of the Egyptian Fathers*

## 67

You need a spiritual pilgrimage.
Begin by closing your mouth.

*—Sayings of the Egyptian Fathers*

## 68

Always to want your own way,
becoming accustomed to having it,
always to seek the easy path—
all this leads straight to depression.
But love, quietness, and contemplation of the inner life
cleanse our hearts.

—*Sayings of the Egyptian Fathers*

## 69

Never look down on anyone.
You do not know whether the spirit of God
prefers to dwell in you or in them.

—*Sayings of the Egyptian Fathers*

## 70

These are the seven rules of a monk:
In the first place, as scripture says,
DEUT. 6:5,
MATT. 22:37
"Love God with all your soul and all your mind."
Then, love your fellow human beings
as you love yourself.
Fast from all evil.

Never pass judgment on anyone, for any cause.
Never do evil to anyone.
Discipline yourself and purge yourself
from material and spiritual evil.
Cultivate a modest and gentle heart.
If you can do all these things
and see only your own faults, not those of others,
the grace of our Lord Jesus Christ
will be with you abundantly.

—*Sayings of the Egyptian Fathers*

## 71

Love is a most holy condition of the soul
in which it values the mystical knowledge of God
above all other existent things.
We cannot enter into such a state of love, however,
if we are still obsessively clinging
to material values.

—*Maximus the Confessor*

## 72

If we believe in the Lord,
we will stand in awe of his judgment,

and this fear of judgment can serve
to rein in our reckless obsessions.
Once we have gained control here,
we should also learn to accept sufferings patiently.
Such acceptance will lead us into a deep hope in God.
This hope in God begins to disconnect our spiritual
    intellect
from all material obsessions.
When our intellect has been liberated,
it will finally possess the love of God.

—*Maximus the Confessor*

# 73

A soul that is yet the victim of its imaginations,
that is driven by obsessive desires
and brimming with animosities,
still stands in need of much purification.

—*Maximus the Confessor*

# 74

If we look inside our hearts
and find there even a trace of animosity toward others

for the wrongs they have done to us,
then we should realize that we are still far removed
from the love of God.
The love of God absolutely precludes us
from hating any human being.

—*Maximus the Confessor*

## 75

If you love God,
you will certainly start to love your neighbors too.
You will find you are unable to hoard your money any
    longer
but will want to distribute it in a godly way,
being generous to all who are in need.

—*Maximus the Confessor*

## 76

If you imitate God by giving alms,
you must not discriminate between
the deserving and the undeserving,
between the wicked and the innocent.
For God gives what is necessary to all

with an open hand, as is appropriate to them,
although he sees the heart's intention
and always honors a good person
more than the wicked.

—*Maximus the Confessor*

## 77

Discipline your flesh with fasting and vigils
and apply yourself assiduously
to the recitation of the Psalter and to prayer,
then the sanctifying gift of self-control
will descend on you,
bringing love with it.

—*Maximus the Confessor*

## 78

Do not listen to gossip
at your neighbor's expense,
and do not spend time talking with
those who love to find fault in others,
otherwise you will fall away from the love of God
and find yourself alienated from the eternal life.

—*Maximus the Confessor*

# 79

Tie the leg of a sparrow to the ground,
and no matter how hard it tries to fly,
it will be fastened to the earth.
In the same way, if your intellect tries to fly up
to the mystical knowledge of heavenly realities
but has not yet been freed of obsessive passions,
it will remain tied fast to the earth.

*—Maximus the Confessor*

# 80

Once the soul starts to feel
how healthy it has become,
it will also notice that even its dreams
have become simplified and calmed.

*—Maximus the Confessor*

# 81

If you are a theologian, you will pray in truth.
If you can pray in truth, then you are a theologian.

*—Evagrios of Pontus*

## 82

When you pray, be concentrated,
without self-display,
closely withdrawn into your heart,
for the demons fear concentration
more than thieves fear dogs.

*—John Klimakos*

## 83

The heart itself is only a small vessel,
yet dragons are there, and lions;
there are poisonous beasts
and all the treasures of evil;
there are rough and uneven roads;
there are precipices;
but there, too, are God and the angels;
life is there, and the Kingdom;
there, too, is light, and there the apostles,
and heavenly cities, and treasures of grace.
All things lie within that little space.

*—Makarios the Great*

## 84

If the souls of disciples are not lit
from the lamp of the Godhead dwelling within,
then what nothings they are.
The Lord was such a "burning lamp"                         JOHN 5:35
because the spirit of the Godhead
dwelled substantially in him
and, in the humanity,[3] set his very heart on fire.

—*Makarios the Great*

## 85

A smelly old pouch can be filled with pearls.
So, too, Christians, in the exterior person,
ought to be humble and of lowly esteem,
but inside, in the secret self,
they possess the "pearl of great price."                    MATT. 13:46

—*Makarios the Great*

## 86

If you feel oppressed,
go into a dimly lit and quiet place.

Lift both your hands up to heaven.
Make the sign of the cross over yourself.
Then lift up the eyes of your soul toward God.
The oppression will leave you.

—*Symeon the New Theologian*

## 87

The first stage of the spiritual life,
the beginning of it all,
is to gain some control over the passions.
The second stage is to devote oneself
to the vocal recitation of the psalms,
for when the passions have been calmed
and prayer has brought some order
in our quest for pleasure,
then the psalms can bring us great delight,
and they are pleasing in God's sight.
The third stage is to pray with our mind.
The fourth is when we ascend to contemplation.

—*Symeon the New Theologian*

## 88

The fathers described prayer as a spiritual weapon
without which we cannot go into battle,

for we would surely be carried off
into exile in enemy country.
But we cannot acquire pure prayer
unless we cling to God with an open heart,
since it is God alone
who gives the gift of prayer to one who prays,
and God who teaches us mystical knowledge.

*—Theodoros the Ascetic*

## 89

It is beyond our power to prevent obsessive thoughts
from troubling and disturbing the soul.
But it is within our power to forbid such imaginings
to linger within
and to forbid such obsessions to control us.

*—Theodoros the Ascetic*

## 90

Withdrawal from the world means two things:
the withering away of our obsessions
and the revelation of the life that is hidden in Christ.  Col. 3:3–4

*—Theodoros the Ascetic*

# 91

The Lord makes his abode
in the souls of the humble,
for the hearts of the proud
are full of shameful obsessions.
Nothing strengthens the obsessions
so much as arrogant thoughts;
nothing uproots the weeds of the soul
so quickly as blessed humility.

—*Theodoros the Ascetic*

# 92

Never let anger or irritability get a grip on you,
for as scripture says:
PROV. 11:25   "The angry man becomes a fool,"
whereas wisdom makes its abode
in the heart of the gentle.

—*Theodoros the Ascetic*

# 93

If you want a life of discipleship,
do not allow the desire for material possessions

to get a grip on you.
A disciple with many possessions
is like a ship that has been too heavily laden.
It is lashed by the storms of cares
and sinks in the deep waters of distress.
The love of money gives birth
to many evil obsessions
and has rightly been called the "root of all evil."  1 TIM. 6:10

—*Theodoros the Ascetic*


## 94

Friend of Christ,
you should seek to have, as your friends,
persons who will be of help to you
in the way of life you want.
Let your friends be lovers of peace,
those who are spiritual soul mates,
and those who are saintly.

—*Theodoros the Ascetic*


## 95

Do not develop a taste for rich and exotic foods. . . .
Make your diet a simple one,

and even then be careful to avoid excess.

As scripture says:

Prov. 24:15
LXX
"Do not be led astray by gluttonous feasting."

—*Theodoros the Ascetic*

# 96

Pray night and day.
Pray when you are happy
and pray when you are sad.
Pray with fear and trembling,
and with a watchful and vigilant mind,
that your prayer might be acceptable to the Lord;
for as scripture says:
"The eyes of the Lord are on the righteous,

Ps. 34:15
and his ears are open to their appeal."

—*Theodoros the Ascetic*

# 97

Love has rightly been called the capital city of all virtues,

Matt. 22:40,
Rom. 13:10
the fulfillment of the Law and the Prophets.
So let us make every effort to attain this holy love.

By means of love we will be liberated
from the tyranny of evil obsessions
and be raised up high to heaven
on the wings of goodness,
and we will even see the face of God,
so far as this is possible for human nature.

—*Theodoros the Ascetic*

## 98

The patriarch Abraham
undertook the labor of hospitality
and sat by his tent door welcoming passersby,                    GEN. 18:1
and his table was open to all comers,
even to the uncouth and the unworthy,
for he set no limitations.
This was why he was counted worthy
to be present at that most wondrous feast,
when he entertained angels and the Master of All.
We too should love to practice openhearted hospitality
so as to welcome not only angels
but even the Lord himself as our guests,
for it was the Lord who told us:
"Insofar as you did it to one of the least of these,
you did it to me."                                              MATT. 25:40

How good it is to be kind to all,
especially those who are unable to repay you.

—*Theodoros the Ascetic*

## 99

If your heart does not accuse you,
either for negligence
or for harboring evil thoughts
or for having rejected a commandment of God,
then indeed you are pure of heart
and worthy to hear those words:
"Blessed are the pure of heart,
MATT. 5:8    for they will see God."

—*Theodoros the Ascetic*

## 100

With a modest mind and a humble heart,
let us repeat over and again
the prayer that the great saint Arsenios
used to offer to the Lord:
"My God, do not abandon me,
though I have done nothing good in your sight,

but because you are compassionate,
grant me the power to make a start."
And how true it is that all our salvation
lies in the mercy, and in the deep love,
that God has for us.

To him be glory, dominion, and worship.

—*Theodoros the Ascetic*

# BOOK TWO

## *Theoretikos*

### A Century of
### Theoretical Chapters

# 1

The second stage of the spiritual life is the illuminative.
This belongs to those whose efforts in holiness
have achieved the first stage of liberation
from obsessive attachments.
It is characterized by spiritual intuition of existent realities,
by contemplation of the inner constitutions of created
  things,
and by the communion of the Holy Spirit.

*—Niketas Stethatos*

# 2

In the illuminative stage,
the spiritual intellect is purified by divine fire;
a psychic opening of the eyes of the heart occurs,
and the Logos is born in us,
who brings mystical discernments of the highest order. . . .
The one who reaches this state
by the intellect's mystical intuition
rides like Elijah in a chariot of fire.

2 Kings
2:11–13

*—Niketas Stethatos*

# 3

Note how scripture says

Lev. 6:12–13  there must always be fire burning on the altar.
Scripture also says you will be called priests of the Lord,
and that text is also addressed to you:
"You are a chosen race, a royal priesthood,

I Pet. 2:9  a people set apart for God."
So, if you are indeed a high priest of God
and wish to perform the priestly functions of your soul,
make sure that the fire never goes out on your altar.

*—Origen of Alexandria*

# 4

If you really wish to achieve spiritual stillness
and to guard your heart successfully,
then let the prayer
"Lord Jesus, have mercy on me"
become one with your breathing,
and in a few days you will see
how it can all be achieved.

*—Hesychios*

# 5

If anyone truly desires to do the will of God
with all their heart,
God will never abandon them
but will constantly guide them along the paths of his will.
If someone really sets their heart on the will of God,
God will find even a little child to illuminate
so as to communicate his will to that person.
But if a person does not truly desire the will of God,
even if they were to go to a prophet,
God would put it into the heart of that prophet
to give a response comparable to the deceit
that was in the seeker's heart.

—*Dorotheos of Gaza*

# 6

Just as someone who has not been illuminated
should not try to speculate on spiritual mysteries,
even so, when the light of the all-holy Spirit
sheds its powerful radiance on someone,
they too should not try to put it into words.
When the soul is drunk with divine love,

it wants only to enjoy the glory of the Lord
with a voice that is rendered silent.

*—Diadochos of Photike*

# 7

When we have successfully blocked
all the gates of the intellect
by means of the remembrance of God,
it is necessary to give the intellect something to do.
We should give it one thing only:
the prayer "Lord Jesus"!
This is more than enough for it,
for it is written that none can say "Jesus is Lord"

I COR. 12:3    except in the Holy Spirit.

Let the spiritual intellect constantly reflect on these words
with great intensity within its inner chambers,
so that it will not be distracted by any mental images.

*—Diadochos of Photike*

# 8

Even in this present time the kingdom of light
and the heavenly icon, our Lord Jesus Christ,

mystically illuminate the soul.
Although he reigns in the souls of his saints,
Christ lies hidden from the eyes of the crowd.
Only with the eyes of the soul can he be seen,
and so will he remain hidden
until the day of resurrection;
but on that day we will be bodily covered
with the light of the Lord,
and our whole being will be radiant,
as our souls are even now.

—*Makarios the Great*


# 9

All God's gifts to us are beyond all beauty
and are the origin of all our goodness,
but there is nothing that can set our hearts on fire
or move them to the love of goodness itself
as much as the gift of divine understanding.
It is the firstborn child of God's grace
and the first of the great gifts he gives to the soul.
It starts by disconnecting us
from our current obsessive desires
and gives us, instead of our longing for corruptible things,
a deepening love for the ineffable riches
of divine comprehensions.

From that point onward,
the mind catches fire in a blaze of transcendence,
so as to become a concelebrant
in the liturgy of the angels.

—*Diadochos of Photike*

# 10

Beloved one,
if you really want to advance your salvation,
you must practice this method of prayer:
Begin with total obedience
and a conscience that is innocent in the sight of God.
Then your mind must keep watch over your heart
during the time you are at prayer,
as if patrolling it all the time.
From the center of your heart,
from the heart's very depths,
your mind should send up its prayer.

—*Symeon the New Theologian*

# 11

As soon as your mind has experienced
what the scripture says:

"How gracious is the Lord,"  Ps. 34:8<br>LXX
it will be so touched with that delight
that it will no longer want to leave the place of the heart.
It will echo the words of the apostle Peter:
"How good it is to be here."  Matt. 17:4

—*Symeon the New Theologian*

## 12

Sometimes people find themselves brightly illuminated
and refreshed by God's grace for a while,
but then this grace may be taken away,
and they can fall into depression and start grumbling
and even give up dispiritedly
instead of energetically renewing their prayers
to call down again that assurance of salvation.
Such behavior is like an ungrateful beggar
taking alms at the palace door
and then walking off indignantly
because he was not invited in
to dine with the king himself.

—*John of Karpathos*

## 13

Scripture says:
"Blessed are those who have not seen

JOHN 20:29 and yet have believed."
Just so, blessed are those who feel that grace
has been withdrawn from them
and no longer find any consolation in their hearts,
only constant tribulation and a dark abyss,
but even so do not give in to despair.
Instead, they take strength from their faith
so as to bear up courageously,
secure in the thought that in this way they are
    experiencing
the vision of the Invisible One.

*—John of Karpathos*


## 14

It is more important to remember God
than it is to remember to breathe.

*—Gregory of Nazianzus*


## 15

Blessed are you, O heart that is lucid,
the dwelling place of the deity.
Blessed are you, O heart that is pure,

which beholds the hidden essence.
Blessed are you, flesh and blood,
the dwelling place of the Consuming Fire.
Blessed are you, mortal body made from dust,
home of the fire that sets the ages alight.

*—Sahdona the Syrian*

## 16

It is truly a matter for wonder and astonishment
that he, before whom even the heavens are not pure
and who fills even his great angels with awe,
should think to take delight and pleasure
in a heart of flesh,
one that is filled with love for him,
and so has become large enough and pure enough
to be his dwelling place.

*—Sahdona the Syrian*

## 17

Those who possess love,
that perfection of the commandments,
become the dwelling place of the Trinity

and can see within their heart
the vision of God.
Blessed is that heart that has deserved to see this sight;
blessed is the heart that has become the home of love
and in which the Godhead has come to dwell.
Such a person, even in this present age,
is living in the Kingdom of Heaven.

—*Sahdona the Syrian*

# 18

Let us embrace the burning fire
of God's love within our hearts,
for the heart's purity is born from our closeness to him.
It is only by unfailing and focused gazing
that the spirit gravitates to God,
but when the luminous ray
of the simple eye of the soul
is flooded with those intense rays of light
that flash down on us from on high,
then it is that the fire of God flares up
in a great blaze within our hearts.

—*Sahdona the Syrian*

# 19

Blessed are you, Lord, who dwell in the heights
and yet have chosen to live within a human heart,
giving it joy and lifting it up
to the heights alongside you,
to live with you there,
to praise you in the heights and in the depths.
Glory to you,
who have given such wonders to a heart
that your own hands made
from the very dust of the earth.

—*Sahdona the Syrian*

# 20

Blessed is that soul whose eye has been cleansed
of all the sorrows of this present age—
those dark storm clouds—
and which has been rendered simple and lucid
so that it can discern the Lord
wrapped in a cloud of light.

—*Sahdona the Syrian*

## 21

You cannot achieve pure prayer
while you are still entangled in material affairs
and agitated by incessant worries,
for prayer is the abandonment of thoughts.

*—Evagrios of Pontus*

## 22

The breast of the Lord:
such is the mystical knowledge of God.
Whoever reclines there
will be a theologian.[4]

*—Evagrios of Pontus*

## 23

Abba Antony said:
I no longer fear God. I have come to love him,
for perfect love casts out fear.

1 John 4:18

*—Apophthegmata Patrum*

# 24

The Kingdom of Heaven
means dispassion of the soul
along with true spiritual insight into existent reality.

*—Evagrios of Pontus*

# 25

The Kingdom of God
is knowledge of the Holy Trinity
filling the whole capacity of the spiritual intellect
and carrying it into incorruptibility.

*—Evagrios of Pontus*

# 26

If you attain mystical knowledge
and experience the delight that rises from it,
no longer will the dark spirit of arrogance
be a seduction for you,
not even if it should offer you
all the kingdoms of the world;                    MATT. 4:8
for what is there, may I ask,

that could possibly surpass
the delight of spiritual contemplation?

—*Evagrios of Pontus*

## 27

You can tell the state of dispassion has been reached
when the spiritual intellect starts to catch glimpses
of its own inner radiance,
when it can remain in a state of tranquillity
even when troubled by dream images,
and when it can look on all of life's affairs
with equanimity.

—*Evagrios of Pontus*

## 28

When the spiritual intellect practices
the ascetic life, with God's help,
and draws near to mystical knowledge,
it ceases to have much, if any,
awareness of the subrational affairs of the soul;
for contemplative knowledge carries it on high
and detaches it from the senses.

—*Evagrios of Pontus*

# 29

Keeping the commandments is not necessarily
the full healing of the soul's powers.
For this, the spiritual intellect
also needs contemplative vision.

*—Evagrios of Pontus*

# 30

Love is the child of dispassion.
Dispassion is the very flower of ascetic practice.
Ascetic practice consists in keeping the commandments.
The guardian of the commandments
is the fear of the Lord.
The fear of the Lord is the child of right faith.
Faith is so innate a good thing,
it can be found even in those
who have not yet learned to believe in God.

*—Evagrios of Pontus*

# 31

Prayer is the conversation
of the spiritual intellect with God.

Imagine what state of spiritual awareness is necessary
to give us the capacity to stand without faltering
in the presence of the Master
and to speak with him face-to-face.

—*Evagrios of Pontus*

## 32

Prayer emanates from joy and thanksgiving.

—*Evagrios of Pontus*

## 33

Prayer is the remedy for sadness and depression.

—*Evagrios of Pontus*

## 34

Once you learn to be patient,
you will always pray in great joy.

—*Evagrios of Pontus*

# 35

Who else is good apart from God?
So, entrust all your life to him
and all will be well with you.

—*Evagrios of Pontus*

# 36

Our God is good,
and most certainly the giver of good gifts.

—*Evagrios of Pontus*

# 37

Do not be upset if you do not immediately receive
what you asked God to give you.
The Lord wants to give you greater things
than you have even thought to pray for—
to teach you to persevere in prayer.

—*Evagrios of Pontus*

# 38

Can you imagine any greater thing
than to have communion with God himself
and to be wholly absorbed by him?

*—Evagrios of Pontus*

# 39

Undistracted prayer
is the highest act of the human intellect.

*—Evagrios of Pontus*

# 40

We try to live honorably
so that we can discern the inner meaning of existent
    things,
and we try to discern that in order to make our way
to the divine Logos in the ontological heart of all things;
for the Logos manifests himself to us
when we are in this state of prayer.

*—Evagrios of Pontus*

# 41

The state of prayer
is a condition transcending material obsessions.
In profound love it carries up the spirit that loves wisdom
to the heights of intelligible reality.

—*Evagrios of Pontus*

# 42

If you pray "in spirit and in truth,"                    John 4:23
you will no longer honor the Creator
because of his works
but will praise him because of himself.

—*Evagrios of Pontus*

# 43

When the mind has divested itself of its fallen state
and has clothed itself with the state of grace,
then in the time of prayer
it can even see its own inner condition,
which is something like a sapphire
or the azure blue of the sky.

Exod. 24:10 Scripture calls this the dwelling place of God,
which the elders saw on Mount Sinai.

—*Evagrios of Pontus*

## 44

When you are praying, do not try to envisage
the Godhead within you in any imagined form.
Do not let your mind be cast in the mold
of any particular figure.
Instead, draw close to the Immaterial One immaterially,
and then you will understand.

—*Evagrios of Pontus*

## 45

There is a text in the Apocalypse
that speaks of an angel who brought incense
Rev. 8:3 and offered it with the prayers of the saints.
In my opinion, this refers to that grace
that the angel makes alive in us
when he brings the mystical knowledge of true prayer,

so that the spirit can henceforth stand firm,
liberated from all agitation, weariness, and carelessness.

—*Evagrios of Pontus*

## 46

The bowls of incense
mentioned in the Apocalypse                               Rev. 5:8
are, we are told, the prayers of the saints,
which are offered up by the twenty-four elders.
The bowl symbolizes the love of God
or, more precisely,
that perfection of spiritual love
in which prayer comes alive "in spirit and in truth."         John 4:23

—*Evagrios of Pontus*

## 47

If you pray truly,
you will discover great confidence,
and angels will come to you
as they once came to Daniel,                              Dan. 2:19

and they will enlighten you
about the inner meaning of created existences.

—*Evagrios of Pontus*

## 48

Just as sight is the most important of all the senses,
so is prayer the most divine of all the virtues.

—*Evagrios of Pontus*

## 49

When you stand in prayer
and feel that no other joy can be compared to it,
then you have indeed discovered true prayer.

—*Evagrios of Pontus*

## 50

How beautiful is a head that is adorned
with a priceless diadem
set with clusters of Indian gemstones and pearls.

But incomparably more beautiful is a soul
that is rich in the knowledge of God
and illuminated by the most radiant contemplation,
for it has the Holy Spirit dwelling within.
Who could ever properly tell of the beauty
of such a blessed soul?

*—Theodoros the Ascetic*

# 51

The fragrance of an expensive perfume,
even when it is kept in its jar,
will permeate every room in a house,
delighting not only the owners
but even the neighbors as well.
So it is with a saintly soul, loved by God,
for its fragrance will emanate
through all the senses of its body,
making known to those who can discern
the holiness that lies hidden within.

*—Theodoros the Ascetic*

# 52

When you are in love,
surely your constant concern

is to be near the beloved
at any and every opportunity,
and you avoid anything that would hinder you
from being in the company and society
of your loved one.
So it is when someone loves God.
One constantly desires
to be with him and speak with him.
This can only be achieved through pure prayer,
so let us apply ourselves to prayer
with all our strength,
for it makes us become like the Lord.
This is the meaning of the scripture that says:
"O God, my God, I cry to you at dawn;

Ps. 63:1
LXX

my soul has thirsted after you."
This person who cries to God at dawn
signifies the spiritual intellect
that has withdrawn from every evil
and that has been wounded to the heart
by the love of God.

—*Theodoros the Ascetic*


## 53

When love carries off the intellect to ecstasy
in mystical knowledge of the Divine
and it stands apart from existent realities,

it then becomes aware of the infinity of God.
It is at that moment, as Isaiah tells us,
that it is utterly outside itself
and comes into a profound sense of its own smallness.
In its wonder it repeats the words of the prophet:
"Alas for me, for I am wounded in the heart.
I am a man of unclean lips,
dwelling among a people of unclean lips,
and I have seen the King, the Lord of Hosts,
with my own eyes."                                    Isa. 6:5

*—Maximus the Confessor*


# 54

Blessed is that spiritual intellect
that travels beyond all existent realities
and comes into the endless delight
of the divine beauty.

*—Maximus the Confessor*


# 55

Do not despise Christ's commandment of love,
for it is the means by which you can become
the child of God.

*—Maximus the Confessor*

## 56

The perfect peace of the holy angels
derives from their two fixed attitudes:
their love of God and their love for each other.
The same applies to the saints of all the ages.
This is why it is most truly said:
"On these two commandments

MATT. 22:40 hang all the Law and the Prophets."

—*Maximus the Confessor*

## 57

A person who has attained such a state of love
that their whole existence is ordered by it
is the one who can say,

1 COR. 12:3 "Jesus is Lord," in the Holy Spirit.

—*Maximus the Confessor*

## 58

The whole purpose of the Savior's commandments
is to liberate the intellect
from its malice and crudeness
and to lead it into his love

and into love of one another.
Out of this love shines
the radiance of mystical knowledge
that God's holy power makes possible in us.

*—Maximus the Confessor*


## 59

If you assiduously concentrate on the interior life,
you will become restrained and patient,
kind and humble.
Then you will also be able to contemplate,
theologize, and pray.
This is what the apostle Paul meant when he said,
"Walk in the Spirit."                                    GAL. 5:16

*—Maximus the Confessor*


## 60

The Savior told us: "Blessed are the pure of heart,
for they will see God,"                                  MATT. 5:8
And they will see him,
and all the treasures he keeps hidden within,
when they have purified themselves

by love and self-control.
The greater their purification,
the clearer their vision.

—*Maximus the Confessor*

## 61

When you have been found worthy
of the contemplation of divine and transcendent realities,
then give your full attention to the refinement of
love and self-control,
for in this way you can guard your unstable
and disturbed soul in all tranquillity
and allow its light to shine out radiantly.

—*Maximus the Confessor*

## 62

Control the soul's restless fluctuations by love.
Calm its desires by self-control.
Give wings to its powers of understanding by prayer.
Then the light of your spiritual intellect
will never be dimmed.

—*Maximus the Confessor*

# 63

Love and self-control
liberate the soul from its obsessions.
Reading and reflection
deliver the intellect from ignorance.
Regular prayer
brings the soul into the very presence of God.

*—Maximus the Confessor*

# 64

God alone is good by nature,
and only the person who imitates God
can be good in moral terms.
Such a person has only one aim in life:
never to fall away from that single goal that matters,
which is our God himself.

*—Maximus the Confessor*

# 65

The soul is like hardening clay
if it clings to materiality.
It is like wax when it clings to God.

It can become like either nature
according to its purpose and intent. . . .
Any soul that clings to God is softened like wax
and receives the impression and seal
of divine realities within it.
In the Spirit it becomes
EPH. 2:22 the very dwelling place of God.

—*Maximus the Confessor*

## 66

Whoever believes, fears.
Whoever fears is humble.
Whoever is humble becomes gentle.
Whoever is gentle
pacifies the unruly forces of desire and aggression
and begins to keep the commandments.
Whoever keeps the commandments is purified.
Whoever is purified is illuminated.
Whoever is illuminated
is made a spouse of the divine Logos-Bridegroom
and shares with him
the bridal chamber of the mysteries.

—*Maximus the Confessor*

## 67

Disciples who seek after mystical knowledge
should call out ceaselessly to God
for their deliverance from evil
and in thanksgiving
for their communion in his blessings.

—*Maximus the Confessor*

## 68

A soul can never attain
to the mystical knowledge of God
unless and until God himself stoops down in mercy
to grasp it and then lift it up to himself.
The spiritual intellect of a human being
lacks this power, of itself,
to ascend and participate in divine illumination.
God must first draw the intellect on high—
insofar as this is possible for the humanity—
and then illuminate it with the rays of divine light.

—*Maximus the Confessor*

## 69

As the Gospel tells us,
by simple faith disciples can move

the mountain of their sinfulness

MATT. 17:20 by the practice of virtue.

This is how we free ourselves

from the restless whirl of existential sensation.

—*Maximus the Confessor*

## 70

If you are able to be a true disciple,

you will receive the fragments of mystical loaves

from the hands of the Logos himself

MATT. 14:19–20 and will feed thousands of people.

—*Maximus the Confessor*

## 71

LEV. 16:31 The "Sabbath of Sabbaths"

signifies the spiritual calm

of the Logos-formed soul,

which has abstracted its intellect

even from the contemplation

of all the godlike principles within existent things.

Such a soul is clothed altogether in God

through an ecstasy of love,

for mystical theology has brought it
to perfect stasis in God himself.

*—Maximus the Confessor*

## 72

The Kingdom is the inheritance
of those who are saved,
their dwelling place and their home,
for such is the tradition the true Logos gave us.
It is the final fulfillment of those who turn
toward the ultimate goal of desire.
Once they have reached this state,
they will be given rest from all motion,
since there will no longer be any time or age
through which they have to pass.
After passing through all things,
they will have come to rest in God,
who is before all ages
and whom the nature of ages cannot contain.

*—Maximus the Confessor*

## 73

You may attain to the highest level of interior life
in your asceticism and your contemplation,

but as long as you still live this present life,

your spiritual knowledge and prophecy

and the pledge of the Holy Spirit

<sub>I COR.</sub> will all be yours "only in part,"

<sub>13:9–12</sub> never completely.

But when you come,

beyond the constricting limit of the ages,

to that perfect condition in which those who are worthy

<sub>I COR. 13:12</sub> see the truth face-to-face, as it truly is,

then you will no longer have only a part of the fullness

but will share in the entire pleroma[5] of grace,

as Saint Paul says:

"according to the measure of the stature

<sub>EPH. 4:13</sub> of the pleroma of Christ."

For in him all the treasures of wisdom

<sub>COL. 2:3</sub> and mystical knowledge lie hidden.

*—Maximus the Confessor*


## 74

The body will be divinized[6] along with the soul

through its own special communion

in the process of deification.

So the One God will be made manifest

in the soul and in the body too,

since he moves them both

beyond their own natural limitations,
through the superabundance of his glory.

—*Maximus the Confessor*

## 75

True love of God, and of divine knowledge,
when it is joined with the soul's renunciation
of its love affair with material embodiment,
is our deliverance from all evil,
and the short road to our salvation.

—*Maximus the Confessor*

## 76

The spiritual intellect
becomes freed from attachment to bodily forms
and transcends the sensation of delight or sorrow
when it is bonded and made one with God,
who is truly all that we long for, desire, and love.

—*Maximus the Confessor*

# 77

The fact that God became a human being
is a firm confirmation of our hope
for the divine transformation of human nature.
Humanity will be made divine
just as God himself became a man.

HEB. 4:15  He who became man without any sin
will deify human nature,
yet without changing it into divine nature,
and he will personally exalt it as high
as he was once brought low for humanity's sake.
This is the mystical teaching
of the great apostle Paul, who said:
"In the age to come he will make manifest

EPH. 2:7  the overflowing riches of his grace."

—*Maximus the Confessor*

# 78

Not every person is able to achieve
the highest state of transcendent soul;
but it certainly is possible
for everyone to find reconciliation with God,
and it is this that will save them.

—*John Klimakos*

# 79

The different forms of virtues
and the inner systems of existent things
are all patterns of divine blessings,
and by means of them
God is continually incarnated.
He is embodied in the form of virtues
and ensouled in the inner systems
of mystical knowledge.
By these means he deifies
those who are found worthy,
stamping in them the seal of true virtue
and giving them the infallible essence
of the mystic knowledge of the truth.

—*Maximus the Confessor*

# 80

God is revealed to each person
in the way they conceptualize the divine glory.
For those who aspire to transcend
the complex structure of matter,
and whose psychic powers are wholly integrated
so as to dance closely around the deity,
he reveals himself as unity and trinity. . . .

For those whose capacities are limited
to the complex structure of materiality
and whose psychic powers are not integrated,
he reveals himself as they are, not as he is,
for they are still caught up in physical conceptions
of the duality of matter and form.

—*Maximus the Confessor*

## 81

The godly apostle Paul
describes the various energies
of the Holy Spirit as varied gifts of grace,
telling us that they all come

I Cor. 12:11  from the single power of the Spirit.
The revelation of the Spirit, however, is given
in the measure of each disciple's faith,
and in the form of communion
in a special gift of grace.
This power of the Spirit
is available for each believer
in a way that corresponds
to the quality of their psychic state
and of their faith and receptivity,
and it is this grace of the Spirit's power

that allows them the capacity
to fulfill the various commandments.

*—Maximus the Confessor*

## 82

You need to gain three things before all others:
The first is freedom from the anxieties of life;
the second is a clear conscience;
the third is complete detachment,
such that your thoughts no longer buzz around
    materialities.
When you have acquired these things,
then sit down by yourself in a quiet place,
out of the way of everyone,
and close the door and withdraw your intellect
from all worthless and transient things.
And pray in this way:
Rest your head down upon your chest
and focus your physical sight
along with the eye of your intellect
upon the center of your stomach, at your navel.
Restrain a little the rhythm
of drawing in breath through your nostrils
so as to allow your intellect
to search inside your inner self

for the place where the heart is,
where all the powers of the spiritual intellect
have their dwelling.
In the beginning you will find only darkness,
dryness, and obscurity.
But if you still persist,
practicing this task attentively night and day,
you will find—and how marvelous it is—
the dawning of unceasing joy.

—*Symeon the New Theologian*


## 83

Once the intellect has accomplished its task
of discovering the place where the heart resides,
it will immediately see things
of which it was previously ignorant
and could never have hoped to find.
It will see the open spaces within the heart
and will see itself as entirely radiant with light
and full of discernment and perception.
When this happens, from whatever source,
thoughts might try to stir up again;
allow none of them to assume
imaginative or syllogistic form within the intellect.
Drive every thought away

with the invocation of the name of Jesus,
saying: "Lord Jesus Christ, have mercy on me."
The rest you will learn for yourself,
with God's help.
But always be sure to keep strict guard
over your intellect
and retain Jesus in your heart
by praying those words:
"Lord Jesus Christ, have mercy on me."

—*Symeon the New Theologian*

# 84

When the love of God is completely overwhelming,
it binds the lover not just to God
but to everyone else too.

—*Thalassios the Libyan*

# 85

Love is the only thing
that can bind together God and his creation
and bring about social harmony.

—*Thalassios the Libyan*

# 86

How precious in the sight of God, and all people,
is a person who tries to live always from love.

—*Thalassios the Libyan*

# 87

Love and self-control purify the soul.
Pure prayer makes the spiritual intellect radiant.

—*Thalassios the Libyan*

# 88

Put a seal on your senses by stillness,
then sit in judgment over the thoughts,
which make a noisy clamor in your heart.

—*Thalassios the Libyan*

# 89

Our Lord and God is Jesus the Christ.
The psychic intelligence of anyone

who follows him
will not remain in darkness.                    JOHN 12:46

                —*Thalassios the Libyan*


# 90

Do not neglect the discipline of Praktikos,
and then your spiritual intellect
will become luminous.
So it is written:
"I will reveal to you unseen and hidden treasures."     IsA. 45:3

                —*Thalassios the Libyan*


# 91

The spiritual intellect that has been liberated
from its obsessions
becomes filled with light,
and ever more illuminated
by the mystical intuition of existent realities.

                —*Thalassios the Libyan*

## 92

Spiritual knowledge is the radiant light of the soul.
Whoever lacks it is the one scripture speaks of:
ECCLES. 2:14 "the fool that walks in darkness."

*—Thalassios the Libyan*

## 93

As soon as the spiritual intellect
has reached full purification,
it will start to feel cramped by its existential limits
and will long to transcend all transient realities.

*—Thalassios the Libyan*

## 94

Blessed are they who have attained to infinite infinity,
for they have transcended all the limits of limitations.

*—Thalassios the Libyan*

## 95

To reach the heights of dispassion
makes even our spiritual reflections dispassionate.

And the heights of mystical knowledge
bring us into the presence
of the One who is beyond all possibility of knowing.

*—Thalassios the Libyan*

# 96

The mystical knowledge
of the holy and consubstantial Trinity
is sanctification and deification
both for humans and for angels.

*—Thalassios the Libyan*

# 97

Those who are still making progress
on the spiritual path
will not yet have achieved stability of attitude.
But those who have reached a perfect stage
can hardly ever be deflected from their path.

*—Thalassios the Libyan*

## 98

Abstract your soul
from the material sensation of sensory things
and your spiritual intellect will find itself in God
and in the world of intellective things.

—*Thalassios the Libyan*

## 99

God is Light,
the Most High, the Unapproachable;
God cannot be conceived in the mind
or spoken by the lips.
God is the Life-Giver for every rational creature.
God is to the world of spiritual intellect,
what the sun is to the sensory world,
and will manifest divinity in our minds
to the degree that we are purified.

—*Gregory of Nazianzus*

## 100

Master, as you looked down upon us once before,
look down upon us again.

As you intended your incarnation for our salvation—
for you came to save us who were lost—
so now do not close us out
of the company of the saved.
Raise up our souls and save our bodies.
Cleanse us all from every wickedness.
Liberate us from our obsessive desires, Lord,
and let us worship you alone in the eternal light.
Let us rise up from the dead
and dance in that blessed, eternal,
and unbreakable ring—
our dancing with the angels.

—*Thalassios the Libyan*

# BOOK THREE

# *Gnostikos*

## A Century of
## Gnostic Chapters

# 1

We ascend through three stages
of development to perfection:
the purgative, the illuminative,
and finally the mystical,
which is perfection itself.
The first is for beginners.
The second is for the more advanced,
and the third is for the perfect.
If we are serious about it,
then we will progress through these three stages,
growing in maturity in Christ
and finally attaining the stature of perfect maturity,
"which is the measure of the stature
of the pleroma of Christ."          EPH. 4:13

—*Niketas Stethatos*


# 2

Just as thoughts enter the heart
only through the mental images of sensory experiences,
so the blessed light of the Godhead
will illumine the heart
only when it has been completely emptied
of all things and stripped of all sensory forms.

Indeed, that brightness is manifested
to the pure intellect
to the same degree it has become void
of all ideational forms.

—*Hesychios*

3

Carbon can engender a burning flame.
So it is with God, who dwells within our hearts
since we have undergone the mystery
of holy baptism;
for when he sees our minds
freed from the winds of evil
and brought to a state of calmness,
sheltered by the guardianship of the intellect,
he is more than ready to kindle our minds
to contemplation—
like a flame lighting a candle.

—*Hesychios*

4

When the heart has acquired stillness,
it will look upon the heights and depths of knowledge,

and the intellect, once quieted,
will be given to hear wonderful things from God.

—*Hesychios*

## 5

God hides the mysteries he offers us
so that he might teach us to search for them in love.

—*Narsai of Edessa*

## 6

There is no radiance greater than the light
of the spirit's initiation;
no wisdom on earth possesses comparable power.
It cannot be measured on the scales
against pearls or precious gems;
no priceless thing can be compared to it;
nothing approaches its inner beauty;
all other beautiful things fail in comparison.
It is more desirable than anything on earth,
and its beauty can even lead the world
captive in desire,
seducing angels and humans alike.

—*Narsai of Edessa*

## 7

Cleanse the mirror of your soul
and the single light will merge with you,
manifesting itself to you as trinity.
Then take the light down into your heart,
and there you will see the Living God.

—*John of Dalyutha*

## 8

The love of God is fiery by nature,
and when it descends in an extraordinary degree
onto a person,
it throws that soul into ecstasy.

—*Isaac of Nineveh*

## 9

A human being cannot possibly see God,
but "things impossible for humans
are possible for God."
And so God can be seen by humans
when he so allows it,
by those he has chosen to see,

LUKE 18:27

and when and how he wills to be seen,
for God is powerful in all things.
In times past he was seen prophetically,
through the Spirit,
and he has also been seen
in the manner of "adoption,"[7]
through the Son's revelation. . . .
In time to come he will be seen
as Father in the Kingdom of Heaven.
The Spirit will prepare human beings
in the Son of God,
and the Son will lead them to the Father,
and the Father will bestow on them
the gift of incorruption for eternal life,
which comes upon all those who look
upon the face of God.
Those who see light are within light
and share the brilliance of the light.
Just so, those who see God are within God
and receive of his splendor,
a radiance of the vision of God that gives us life.

—*Irenaeus of Lyons*


# 10

The expectation of future blessings
links the spiritual intellect with what it hopes for.

When it dwells continually on these blessings,
it becomes forgetful of present realities.

*—Thalassios the Libyan*


# 11

Jesus is the Christ,
one of the Holy Trinity,
and you will become no less than his heir.

*—Thalassios the Libyan*


# 12

When the spiritual intellect
is stripped of its obsessions,
it discovers the Holy Spirit,
and in the same way, the Spirit initiates it
into the fullness of its hopes.

*—Thalassios the Libyan*


# 13

When the spiritual intellect
begins to practice divine wisdom,

it makes its start with faith.

Then it passes through the intermediate stages,
until it arrives at faith once again,
though this time it is of the most exalted kind.

*—Thalassios the Libyan*

# 14

The ways of God
that the saints can see in contemplation
reveal not the divine self but the divine character.

*—Thalassios the Libyan*

# 15

Why did Christ lead his disciples
onto a high mountain
when he was transfigured in light before them?
It was to show that when disciples arrive
at the summit of love,
they stand out of themselves
and perceive the Invisible One.
Such a person flies over the obscuring clouds
and comes out into the clear sky of the soul,

and so is able to look more acutely
into the sun of righteousness,
although the perfect vision of the Godhead
always transcends our capacities.
On that day pray in solitude.
For stillness is the mother of prayer,
and prayer is the revelation of the glory of God.

*—John of Damascus*

## 16

If you really long for mystical knowledge,
the certain assurance of salvation,
then first make a concentrated effort
to break the soul's obsessive bondage to its body;
strip the soul of the garments
of attachment to materiality
and then let it dive down naked
into the depths of humility,
for it is there you will find
the precious pearl of your salvation,
hidden in the shell of divine knowledge.

*—Theognostos the Priest*

# 17

When you are no longer
at the mercy of your obsessions
and you feel the love of God
burning ever more deeply in your heart,
when you come to the stage
when the thought of death
no longer fills you with dread—
for you look on it merely as a dream of the night
or, more to the point, as a welcome liberation—
then you have indeed found the pledge
of your salvation.
On that day you will be filled with ineffable joy,
for you carry the Kingdom of God within you.

—*Theognostos the Priest*

# 18

I will tell you something strange,
and you must not be alarmed by it.
There is a certain mystery that takes place
between the soul and God
when the soul has reached the highest stages
of purity, faith, and love.
When the disciple reaches final reconciliation,

a unification with God takes place,
for he inhabits the soul
through unceasing prayer and contemplation.
Elijah was in such a union

1 Kings 17:1    when he shut the heavens and made the drought,

Exod. 14:21    and so was Moses, who divided the sea
or conquered Amalek

Exod. 17:11    by simply stretching out his hands,
and so was Jonah when he came out safe

Jon. 2:1–10    from the depths of the sea and the whale.

*—Theognostos the Priest*

# 19

Our God loves humanity most profoundly,
and the disciple who reaches such a state of union
finds that God will refuse him nothing at all.

*—Theognostos the Priest*

# 20

Always wait patiently,
with your faith made active by love,
until God has given you the illumination

to allow you to teach.
There is nothing so sad
as an intellect engaged in theology
when it is devoid of God.

—*Diadochos of Photike*

# 21

Those who meditate unceasingly
upon the holy and glorious name [of Jesus]
in the depths of their heart
can sometimes see the radiance
of their own spirit-intelligence.
For when the mind is profoundly concentrated
on this invocation,
we feel experientially how it starts burning off
all the layer of dirt that normally suffocates the soul.

—*Diadochos of Photike*

# 22

If you can feel the love of God in your heart,
know that you are indeed known by God.
Inasmuch as we experience the sensation

of the love of God in our hearts,
we have truly entered into the love of God.
From that point onward,
we cannot stop longing with all our hearts
for the enlightenment of mystical knowledge,
until such time as we can feel it
entering our very bones
to transform us utterly.

—*Diadochos of Photike*

## 23

Sometimes the soul is set on fire
with the love of God
with a force that moves unerringly, but invisibly,
so that even the body is, as it were,
swept along into the abyss of that unspeakable love.
We can experience the force of that holy grace
when we are most vigilant, or even,
as I have spoken of on other occasions,
in the way that sleep starts to affect us.
But when you feel this movement,
know for certain—
and it is a point of utmost importance—
that it is the motion of the Holy Spirit of God within us.

—*Diadochos of Photike*

# 24

In the early stages,
grace normally enlightens the soul in such a way
that it has a deep sense of its own inner radiance,
but as the soul is advanced
along the difficult path of enlightenment,
it normally communicates its many intimate mysteries
in a manner transcending sensation.

*—Diadochos of Photike*

# 25

The king's treasure chamber is full of gold.
The mind of the true disciple
is full of spiritual knowledge.

*—John of Karpathos*

# 26

The fire of your prayer
ascends to even greater heights
while you meditate on the holy oracles of the Spirit.

Let that fire burn as an eternal flame
on the altar of your soul.

*—John of Karpathos*

## 27

Sit still in prayer
and keep your attention fixed within
so that you may make good progress in holiness
and close yourself off to wickedness.
Because when you are alive to mystical knowledge
    in this way,
you will receive a great abundance
of contemplative insights into so many things.
If you ascend even higher,
the light of our Savior will shine on you
with even greater radiance.

*—Evagrios of Pontus*

## 28

Our rational nature had become dead
through wickedness,
but Christ raised it to life again

by means of the contemplation of all the aeons.
And Christ's Father raises up
the soul that has died in Christ
by means of the spiritual knowledge
that he gives of himself.
This is the meaning of that text of Paul's:
"It is our belief that if we have died with Christ,
we shall also live with him."

2 TIM. 2:11

—*Evagrios of Pontus*


## 29

By prayer the disciple can become
the equal of angels,
who long to "see the face of the Father
who is in heaven."

MATT. 18:10

—*Evagrios of Pontus*


## 30

Do you really long to pray?
Then leave behind present transitory things
and live your life as if you were in heaven—
not just theoretically,

but truly, by angelic actions
and mystical knowledge even more divine.

—*Evagrios of Pontus*

## 31

Faith is the beginning of love.
Mystical knowledge of God
is the perfection of love.

—*Evagrios of Pontus*

## 32

Ps. 68:34   As it is written: "God's glory rests on Israel."
This means, rests upon an intellect that,
so far as this is possible,
contemplates the beauty
of the glory of God himself.
And the text goes on:

Ps. 68:34   "And his power is in the clouds,"
which refers to how the Father
manifests the Beloved,
who sits at his right hand,
to luminous souls who have fixed their eyes

on the dawning light,
and how he floods them with light,
just as the sunlight suffuses the pure white clouds.

*—Hesychios*


# 33

Once the heart has been perfectly emptied of mental
   images,
it gives birth to divine and mystical concepts that play
   within it
just as fish and dolphins play in a calm sea.
As the sea is rippled when a soft breeze moves over it,
so is the heart's abyss moved by the Holy Spirit.
As it is written:
"Because you are sons,
God has sent the Spirit of his Son
into your hearts, crying out: Abba, Father."                    GAL. 4:6

*—Hesychios*


# 34

If the prayer "Lord Jesus, have mercy on me"
is constantly on your mind and on your lips,

and the name is always in your heart
in the way that air circulates in our bodies
or wax feeds the candle flame,
how happy it will make you.
The sun, as it rises over the earth, brings day,
and the holy and venerable name of the Lord Jesus,
when it begins to shine continually in our minds,
produces countless mystical understandings,
all as bright as sunlight.

*—Hesychios*

## 35

When the clouds are dispersed,
how clear the air becomes;
and when our illusory obsessions are dispersed
by that sun of righteousness, Jesus the Christ,
then radiant and star-bright perceptions
come to birth within our hearts,
for Jesus illuminates our atmosphere.
It is what the Wisdom of Solomon speaks of:
"Those who trust in the Lord
will comprehend the truth.
Those who are faithful in love
will dwell with him."

Wisd. of
Sol. 3:9

*—Hesychios*

# 36

The mystical vision
[of the cherubim and living beings]
that Ezekiel saw                 EZEK. 1:4–2:1
was true and accurate and fundamental.
It was the symbolic foretelling of a divine
and mystical reality,
that very "mystery hidden from generations
and from aeons"                 COL. 1:26
that "has been revealed in these last times"     1 PET. 1:20
in the appearing of Christ;
for the prophet was psychically witnessing
the mystery of the human soul
that receives its Lord within
and becomes his throne of glory.

—*Makarios the Great*

# 37

The soul that is found worthy
to participate in the Holy Spirit
and be illuminated by his radiance,
and the ineffable glory of his beauty,
becomes his throne and his dwelling place.
Such a soul becomes all light, all face, all eye
[as in Ezekiel's vision].          EZEK. 1:4–2:1

The soul becomes entirely covered
with the spiritual eyes of light;
nothing in it is left in shadow.

—*Makarios the Great*

## 38

When the soul becomes totally radiant
and covered with the ineffable beauty
of the glory of the light of Christ,
it comes to share in the very life of the divine Spirit
to such perfection that it is changed
into the very chamber and throne of God.

—*Makarios the Great*

## 39

The souls of the righteous become heavenly lights,
as the Lord himself told his apostles:
MATT. 5:14    "You are the light of the world."
And it was he who first transformed them in light,
that through them he might enlighten the cosmos.

—*Makarios the Great*

# 40

If you have become the throne of God,
if the heavenly charioteer has ascended within you
and your soul has become as a single spiritual eye
and has become completely luminous,
and if you have been clothed in light ineffable
and fed from spiritual delights
and drunk from living water,
and all your inner life has been tested
and proven in hope,
then in all truth you have started to live
the eternal life,
even in this present age,
and your soul has found its rest in God.

*—Makarios the Great*

# 41

The Lord clothes his chosen souls in
the garments of the ineffable light of his kingdom,
the garments of faith, hope, love, joy, and peace,
the garments of goodness and kindness
and all comparable things.
They are divine garments
pulsating with light and life,

and they bring us peace that passes all description;
for God is himself Love and Joy and Peace
and Kindness and Goodness,
and this is exactly how he renews our very being
in his grace.

—*Makarios the Great*

## 42

When a soul is full of expectant longing,
and full of faith and love,
God considers it worthy to receive
<sub></sub>Acts 1:8, "the power from on high,"
2:1–3 which is the heavenly love of the spirit of God
and the heavenly fire of immortal life;
and when this happens, the soul truly enters
into the beauty of all love
and is liberated from its last bonds of evil.

—*Makarios the Great*

## 43

Let us strive to seek after that supreme good
that the Lord spoke to us about,

and let us desire this with great longing
so that we may enter into the ineffable love of the Spirit
that Saint Paul advised us to strive after
when he told us to "seek after love." 1 Cor. 14:1
In this way we will be turned from our hardness of heart
by the right hand of the Most High
and be made worthy to come into the day;
our spirits finding their rest
and their deepest delight
when they are wounded by the love of God.
For the Lord greatly loves humankind
and is deeply moved whenever human beings,
in their inmost self, turn wholly to him.

*—Makarios the Great*


## 44

Even worldly persons desire to be associated
with the glory of an earthly king.
How much more true is this of those
whom the finger of the divine Spirit of Life has touched.
Divine love has wounded their hearts
with the longing for Christ,
the true and heavenly King.
His beauty and ineffable glory,
his unfailing graciousness,

and his incomprehensible majesty
have conspired to hold them captive
with desire and longing.
Their whole being is fixed upon him.

—*Makarios the Great*


## 45

How should we believe?
In what way should we struggle
and give all our energy to living a good life?
We should do it with great hope and perseverance
so that we can be found worthy
to receive the power given from heaven
and so receive the glory of the Holy Spirit
in the innermost depths of the soul.

—*Makarios the Great*


## 46

When God created Adam,
he did not give him physical wings
such as the birds had,
for he preferred to give him the wings

of the Holy Spirit.
These he will return to him at the Resurrection,
to raise him up and bear him
wherever the Spirit desires.
It is these wings that even now the saints possess,
so that their spirits can fly up
to the kingdom of heavenly comprehensions.

*—Makarios the Great*

# 47

Sometimes the flame [of a lamp]
can leap up and burn furiously.
At other times it burns gently and quietly.
Sometimes its light leaps up
and emits a great radiance.
At other times its small flame
gives out only a dim light.
This is how it is with the lamp [of grace in the soul].
It is always lit and giving off illumination,
but when it burns with special radiance,
it is as if the soul were drunk with love for God.
At other times, as God himself decides,
the light is still there but is only a dim glow.

*—Makarios the Great*

## 48

The beloved of God
seeks to be consecrated entirely to the Lord
and to cling to him alone,
so as to walk in the way of his commandments
and reverence the overshadowing presence
of the spirit of Christ,
until he becomes one spirit with the Lord,
1 COR. 6:17    as the apostle says.

*—Makarios the Great*

## 49

When the face of the soul has been unveiled,
it will gaze upon the heavenly Bridegroom
face-to-face,
illuminated by the unspeakable light of the Spirit. . . .
On that day the soul is worthy of the heavenly life
and becomes the bright dwelling place
of the spirit of God.

*—Makarios the Great*

## 50

When we start off learning to write,
we first master the written signs

and soon excel in them.
Then we go to a higher school
and find ourselves at the bottom of the class again,
but soon we make progress
until once more we excel,
and then go on to a higher school
and find ourselves at the bottom again,
until once more we learn to excel. . . .
This issue of making progress is just the same,
even more so in the case of the heavenly mysteries:
they allow for great degrees of progress
and many stages of advancement.
Through much application and much practice,
the learner can arrive at perfection.
This is the condition of those Christians
who have truly tasted of God's grace
and bear the sign of the cross
within their minds and hearts . . .
so that they understand
the illusion of material reality.

—*Makarios the Great*

# 51

The Lord is the master silversmith,
who fashions our hearts like embossed silver,

making them new in secret
and lifting them out in relief from the body.
Then the true beauty of the soul is made manifest

—*Makarios the Great*

## 52

Christians who have come to this perfection,
who have been found worthy
to come into full perfection
so as to become the companions of the King,
are those who are unfailingly dedicated
to the Cross of Christ.
Just as in the time of the prophets,
sacred chrism[8] was regarded as the most precious of
　　things,
since both kings and prophets were anointed with it,
so it is now with spiritual disciples,
for they are anointed with heavenly chrism
and become Christs by grace,
for in this way they are kings and prophets
of heavenly mysteries.
They are the children of God,
and as such they are princes and gods.

—*Makarios the Great*

# 53

One who has found and taken possession
of the heavenly treasure of the Spirit inside the heart
is enabled by it to fulfill all the righteousness
of the commandments
and to practice all the virtues
faultlessly and blamelessly.
After that gift,
everything becomes straightforward and easy.

—*Makarios the Great*

# 54

Those who are worthy
to "become the children of God"          John 1:12
and to be "born from on high,"           John 3:3
who have Christ within their hearts,
shining in them radiantly
and giving them peace . . .
are like guests at a royal banquet,
so excited and so full of rejoicing
and unspeakable happiness.
At other times they are like the bride
resting in the secret chamber of the Bridegroom,
sharing the divine repose.

At other times they are like the bodiless angels,
for even their bodies seem to be light and transcendent.
And sometimes it is as if they had been made drunk
with strong wine.
They are inebriated in the Spirit,
intoxicated by divine and spiritual mysteries.

*—Makarios the Great*


## 55

Sometimes the soul finds rest
in the deepest quietness,
and joy and perfect peace
in perfectly focused spiritual delight
and ineffably deep repose.
At other times the soul is stirred up by grace
and taught lessons in ineffable wisdom
and understanding
and knowledge of the spirit,
in ways that pass beyond all our ability
to speak about them. . . .
Manifold are the patterns of grace,
and most varied are the ways it leads the soul.
Sometimes, as God decides,

grace gives rest to the soul.
At other times it puts it to work.

—*Makarios the Great*

## 56

The disciple who progresses entirely
into the ambit of grace becomes sanctified
and thereby advances into complete union
with the Spirit.
Then the disciple is truly rendered holy and pure
by that Spirit,
and is made fit for the Kingdom of God.

—*Makarios the Great*

## 57

For some, the charisms[9] and gifts of the Holy Spirit
are given as an advance.
Some disciples enter into them through faith and prayer,
apparently without any work or grief or toil,
and even while they are still engaged
in the affairs of ordinary life.

Even so, God does not give his grace carelessly
or inappropriately or accidentally
but always in his ineffable and inscrutable wisdom
so that he can test the autonomy and free will
of the disciples
who have come into such grace so unexpectedly.

—*Makarios the Great*


## 58

Let us make our body an altar of sacrifice.
Let us place all our desires on it
and beseech the Lord
that he would send down from heaven
that invisible and mighty fire
to consume the altar and everything that is on it.

—*Makarios the Great*


## 59

Let us be like a crafty merchant
who would never dream of investing exclusively
in only one form of enterprise
but expends his efforts extensively

in the cause of maximizing his assets.
This is exactly how we should develop our soul,
to be versatile and speculative,
so that we can gain a true and great profit,
no less than God, who will teach us himself
how to pray in truth.
For the Lord finds his repose
in the good intent of the soul
and will make it into the throne of the divine glory.

—*Makarios the Great*

# 60

Scrutinize your heart to see if your soul
has taken the Lord as its guiding light,
its true food and drink.
If it has not, then strive eagerly night and day
in order to achieve this.
When you look to the sun,
make sure it is the true sun that you seek,
for remember you are blind.
So when you look into your soul,
see if you can see there a good and true light. . . .
It was Jesus who came to give sight
back to the inner self.

—*Makarios the Great*

## 61

The eyes of the body can see
all things with perfect lucidity.
So it is with the saints,
for to them all the beauties of the Godhead
are clearly visible.

—*Makarios the Great*

## 62

Many lamps can be lit from one fire,
and each one will shine out
with the same nature of light.
So it is when Christians are enkindled
from that one nature and one divine fire,
which is the Son of God.
Then the lamps of their hearts are lit
and burn brightly before him on the earth.
This is why it is said:
"And so God, your God,
Ps. 45:7    has anointed you with the oil of gladness."

—*Makarios the Great*

# 63

The soul that truly believes in Christ
must be transformed and changed
from this present evil condition
to another state, one that is purely good,
and from the present lowly nature
to another, divinized nature.
The disciple will be made completely new
by the power of the Holy Spirit,
and so will be made ready even here
for the heavenly kingdom.

—*Makarios the Great*

# 64

All things are possible for God.
Such was the case of the thief [on the cross].   LUKE
In one moment he was converted through his faith   23:42–43
and was restored to paradise.
It was for this that the Lord came,
so that he might change our souls, re-create them,
and as scripture says,
"make us sharers in the divine nature."   2 PET. 1:4
He will give to our soul a heavenly soul,

which is the Holy Spirit,
who will lead us into the fullness of virtue,
so that we will even start to live the eternal life,
as far as this is now possible.

*—Makarios the Great*

## 65

The sun is in the heavens,
though all the power and radiance of its light
shines on the earth.
So it is with the Lord,
who sits at the right hand of the Father,
EPH. 1:21    "above every principality and power,"
but whose eye looks down
into the hearts of his disciples on earth,
so as to raise up all those who need his help
to where he himself is.
This is why he says:
JOHN 12:20    "For where I am, there shall my servant be also."

*—Makarios the Great*

## 66

The soul that has had the veil of darkness
removed from it by the power of the Holy Spirit,

and whose spiritual eyes have been illuminated
by the heavenly light,
and that has been perfectly liberated
from its unworthy obsessions
and purified by grace,
will at last be able to serve the Lord totally,
in heaven and in the spirit and even in the body.
Such a soul becomes so extensive in its consciousness
that it finds itself everywhere,
wherever it pleases to be;
and wherever it finds itself,
its fundamental desire is to serve the Christ.

*—Makarios the Great*


# 67

Even in this life
the Lord reveals himself to the soul
and is discovered by it,
in knowledge and wisdom and love and faith. . . .
He placed within the soul
understanding and comprehension, volition
and the overseeing guidance of the spiritual intellect,
and he established within it
a great and different kind of subtlety.
For God made the soul able to move wherever it wills,

made it something that is both volatile and inexhaustible.
He gave the soul grace to come and go in an instant,
and to serve him in all the range of its intellective powers,
in whatever place the Spirit wishes.
In short, he made the soul like this
so that it could be his own bride,
and that it might have communion with the Divine,
to be merged in union with God,
and so become as one spirit with God.
It is as scripture says:
"Whoever is joined to the Lord

1 Cor. 6:17    is made one spirit with him."

*—Makarios the Great*


## 68

The Spirit, taking possession of the soul,

Ps. 33:3    sings a new song to the Lord
with the timbrel of the body
and the rational strings of the lyre,
which is the soul . . .
and so it sends up praises to the life-giving Christ.
As breath sounds when passed through a flute,
so does the Holy Spirit make music
in the holy and God-bearing saints,

who sing hymns and psalms to God
from a pure heart.

—*Makarios the Great*


# 69

It was God's own desire
to have communion with the human soul,
and this was why he espoused it to himself
as a royal bride
and why he purified it from all uncleanness.

—*Makarios the Great*


# 70

What did the Lord mean when he said:
"Blessed are the pure in heart,
for they shall see God"?                              MATT. 5:8
Or again when he said:
"Be perfect as your heavenly Father is perfect"?     MATT. 5:48
Did he not promise to us in these words
a state of final purification from all wickedness?
And is this not the final setting aside
of our ignoble obsessions

and our ascent to the perfections
of the highest plane of virtues,
which is itself the ultimate purification
and sanctification of our heart
by means of its communion
with the divine and perfect spirit of God?

—*Makarios the Great*

## 71

As the Apostle said:
"A virgin can devote all her attentions

I COR. 7:34   to the things of the Lord."
This is like the soul trying to be holy
not merely in body but even in spirit,
at every level of thinking and acting,
both openly and in secret,
so that it will be freed of the last vestiges of sin.
For then, with great longing
it will desire, as the bride of Christ,
to be made one with its heavenly King,
to be so united with him
in all his radiant and immaculate beauty
that it becomes as one spirit with him.

—*Makarios the Great*

# 72

Those who truly believe
in the promise of the Spirit
can see most clearly, from many indications,
that it is absolutely necessary
to come to God wholeheartedly
and fully believing in his promises,
and with all our energy
trying to fulfill his commandments.
Day by day, as our inner attitudes
become progressively renewed,
we will grow ever more aware,
in our inmost self,
of the active grace of our spiritual advancement.
This is how we will finally be able to attain
that true repose of perfect sanctification,
which is to say perfect love,
in which we venerate the Spirit
as true children of God.

—*Makarios the Great*

# 73

Christ called that radiance
in which he shone before the apostles            MATT. 17:2

the "Kingdom of the Father."
As he himself said, it is that very Kingdom of God
that comes in power to those who have seen him.
On that day the saints will shine
with radiance and glory,
they will be made scintillatingly bright
by receiving that light
as he gives it to them.
For it is this bread, his body—
which in the present life we come to the altar to receive—
that one day will be revealed to the eyes of all

MATT. 24:30   coming upon the clouds.
In one instant it will display its brilliance
to the east and the west
like a lightning flash.

—*Nicholas Cabasilas*

## 74

The saints of God already live within this radiance,
and at death the light does not depart from them.
The saints possess this light constantly,
and they enter into new life radiant with it.

—*Nicholas Cabasilas*

# 75

Through the sacramental mysteries,
as through windows,
the Sun of Righteousness enters a darkened world. . . .
He introduces the eternal and immortal life
into this failing and dying cosmos
and he lifts it up to transcendence,
for the Life of the World
has overcome the world. . . .                          JOHN 16:33
When the rays of the sun stream into a house,
one hardly notices the lamp any longer
because the radiance of the sun has drowned it out.
Just so, when the brightness of the future life
enters our soul in this present existence
and dwells within it,
it overwhelms our life in the flesh
and all the beautiful allurements of the world
with its own encompassing brightness—
which is our life in the Spirit.

—*Nicholas Cabasilas*

# 76

What is this awesome mystery
that is taking place within me?

I can find no words to express it;
my poor hand is unable to capture it
in describing the praise and glory that belong
to the One who is above all praise,
and who transcends every word. . . .
My intellect sees what has happened,
but it cannot explain it.
It can see, and wishes to explain,
but can find no word that will suffice;
for what it sees is invisible and entirely formless,
simple, completely uncompounded,
unbounded in its awesome greatness.
What I have seen is the totality recapitulated as one,
received not in essence but by participation.
Just as if you lit a flame from a flame,
it is the whole flame you receive.

—*Symeon the New Theologian*


# 77

My Christ,
you are the Kingdom of Heaven,
you are the land promised to the meek,
you are the meadows of paradise,
the hall of the celestial banquet,
the ineffable bridal chamber,

the table open for all comers.
You are the bread of life,
the wonderful new drink,
the cool jar of water,
the water of life.
You are the lamp
that never goes out for all your saints,
the new garment, the diadem,
the one who distributes diadems.
You are our joy and repose,
our delight and glory.
You are gladness and laughter, my God.
Your grace, the grace of the all-holy Spirit,
shines in the saints like a blazing sun.

—*Symeon the New Theologian*

# 78

By what boundless mercy, my Savior,
have you allowed me to become a member of your body?
Me, the unclean, the defiled, the prodigal.
How is it that you have clothed me
in the brilliant garment,
radiant with the splendor of immortality,
that turns all my members into light?
Your body, immaculate and divine,

is all radiant with the fire of your divinity,
with which it is ineffably joined and combined.
This is the gift you have given me, my God:
that this mortal and shabby frame
has become one with your immaculate body
and that my blood has been mingled
with your blood.
I know, too,
that I have been made one with your divinity
and have become your own most pure body,
a brilliant member, transparently lucid,
luminous and holy.
I see the beauty of it all. I can gaze on the radiance.
I have become a reflection of the light of your grace.

*—Symeon the New Theologian*


## 79

The solitary is innocent of the world
and continually speaks with God alone.
He sees him and is seen by him.
He loves him and is loved by him,
and so becomes light itself,
since he is enlightened
in a manner past all speech.

*—Symeon the New Theologian*

# 80

In the midst of that night, in my darkness,
I saw the awesome sight of Christ
opening the heavens for me.
And he bent down to me and showed himself to me
with the Father and the Holy Spirit
in the thrice holy light—
a single light in three, and a threefold light in one,
for they are altogether light,
and the three are but one light.
And he illumined my soul
more radiantly than the sun,
and he lit up my mind,
which had until then been in darkness.
Never before had my mind seen such things.
I was blind, you should know it, and I saw nothing.
That was why this strange wonder
was so astonishing to me,
when Christ, as it were, opened the eye of my mind,
when he gave me sight, as it were,
and it was him that I saw.
He is Light within Light, who appears
to those who contemplate him,
and contemplatives see him in light—
see him, that is, in the light of the Spirit. . . .
And now, as if from far off,
I still see that unseeable beauty,

that unapproachable light, that unbearable glory.

My mind is completely astounded.

I tremble with fear.

Is this a small taste from the abyss,

which like a drop of water

serves to make all water known

in all its qualities and aspects? . . .

I found him, the One whom I had seen from afar,

Acts 7:55–56 the one whom Stephen saw

when the heavens opened,

Acts 9:3–9 and later whose vision blinded Paul.

Truly, he was as a fire in the center of my heart.

I was outside myself, broken down, lost to myself,

and unable to bear the unendurable brightness of that

glory.

And so, I turned

and fled into the night of the senses.

—*Symeon the New Theologian*


# 81

Love came down, as is its way,

in the appearance of a luminous cloud.

I saw it fasten on me and settle upon my head.

And it made me cry out, for I was so afraid;

and so it flew away and left me alone.

Then how ardently I searched after it;
and suddenly, completely,
I was conscious of it present in my heart,
like a heavenly body.
I saw it like the disk of the sun. . . .
It closed me off from the visible
and joined me to invisible things.
It gave me the grace to see the Uncreated.

—*Symeon the New Theologian*

## 82

Grace me with the vision of your face, O Word,
with the enjoyment of your ineffable beauty.
Allow me to contemplate and find my delight
in your vision—ineffable vision, invisible vision,
awesome vision . . .
the reflection of your divine glory,
which allows itself to be seen as a simple light,
a light most sweet.

—*Symeon the New Theologian*

## 83

Do not say it is impossible
to receive the divine Spirit.

Do not say that without him
it is possible to be saved.
Do not say that one can possess the Spirit
though unaware of it.
Do not say that God cannot be seen by human beings.
Do not say that humans can never see the light of God,
or that at least it is not possible for this generation.
My friends, it is never impossible.
It is more than possible for those who desire it.

—*Symeon the New Theologian*

## 84

God heard my cries
and from unimaginable heights stooped down
and looked upon me.
Once more he had pity on me
and allowed me to see
the One who is invisible to all,
so far as this is possible for humankind.
Seeing him I was astounded,
I who was closed up in my tiny house,
confined within such a tiny vessel,
all about surrounded by darkness,
the darkness of the heaven and earth, that is. . . .
I saw him again, but now in the very center

of my tiny house, my tiny vessel.
So quickly had he come there, all completely,
uniting himself to me inexpressibly,
joining himself to me ineffably,
suffusing himself in me unconfusedly,
in the way that fire permeates iron
or light shines though crystal.
So he made me become like fire itself,
revealing himself to me as Light.

—*Symeon the New Theologian*


# 85

It was God who said: Let there be light.     Gen. 1:3
And all at once there was light.
So, if he shines as light
spiritually within a heart
or appears as a flash of light
or as the mighty sun,
what do you think he can do
if he illuminates the soul of a disciple?
Can he not enlighten it
so that it has a clear and perfect understanding of God,
and how he is present within it?

—*Symeon the New Theologian*

## 86

I was in the world like a blind man,
like an atheist, ignorant of my God,
but you yourself had pity on me
and looked down on me
and turned me back to yourself.
You caused your light to shine
so brightly in my darkness
and called me back to you, my maker.

—*Symeon the New Theologian*

## 87

You alone are uncreated, my Savior,
you alone are without beginning. . . .
Holy and all-venerable Trinity,
God of all that is:
you have shown to us the light
of your immaculate glory.
Grant it to me even now, and unceasingly,
my Savior.
Through the light, let me ever contemplate you,
Holy Word,
and begin to see your transcendent beauty.

—*Symeon the New Theologian*

# 88

God is dispassionate spirit-intellect,
transcending every intellect and all dispassion.
God is light, the spring of all blessed light.
God is wisdom, intelligence,
and mystical knowledge.
God is the giver of wisdom, intelligence,
and mystical knowledge.
Those who receive these gifts
on account of their innocence,
those in whom they are abundantly manifested,
are indeed the children of God,
since the icon of God has been preserved
in their innermost selves.

—*Niketas Stethatos*

# 89

If you seek after God with all your heart
and all your strength,
then the virtues of your soul and body
will turn you into a mirror
of the image of God within.
You will be so merged in God,
and God so merged in you,

that each will endlessly repose in the other.
Such are the riches of the gifts of the Spirit
that such a disciple will be, and be manifested as,
the very icon of divine blessedness,
a very god by adoption,
since God is the perfector of his own perfection.

—*Niketas Stethatos*

# 90

Our spiritual intellect is an icon of God,
and it rests in its proper home
when it dwells among its own kind of realities
and when it never deviates
from its proper dignity and condition.
This is why it always loves to rest
among the things of God
and ever seeks to unite itself to God,
who is its origin, its energy,
and who draws it ever upward.

—*Niketas Stethatos*

# 91

Souls that are purified and illuminated
by the rays of primordial light

in a radiance of mystical knowledge
are not only filled with every goodness and luminosity
but carried up to the intellective heavens
through the contemplation of natural essences.
The action of the divine energy
does not stop here, however, but continues until
it has finally made them one with the One
through wisdom and mystical knowledge
of ineffable things,
making them abandon their former multiplicity
and become one in themselves.

*—Niketas Stethatos*

## 92

When you become aware of the increasing fire
of your love for God and inner faith in him,
then you should realize
that you are bringing Christ to birth
within your soul.
It is he who is lifting your soul
high above its earthly and visible limitations
and preparing a dwelling place for it in the heavens.
When you experience your heart filled with joy
and consumed with yearning
for God's ineffable blessings,

then know that the divine Spirit
is working within you.
When you feel your intellect filled with ineffable light
and spiritual understandings of transcendent wisdom,
then recognize that the Paraclete[10]
is actively present in your soul,
uncovering the treasures of the Kingdom of Heaven
that lie hidden within it.

—*Niketas Stethatos*

## 93

In the first ranks of the highest angelic powers,
some circle with eternal motion
around the divine presence,
burning with fire and gazing clear-sightedly
on the Godhead,
while others contemplate God in mystical wisdom,
since this is that divine condition
that sets them in endless revolution around the deity.
It is the same with souls
who have become like the angels.
They too burn with fire for God and are clairvoyant,
advanced in wisdom, in spiritual knowledge,
and in mystical perception.
As God affords them, in their limited way,

these souls also wheel endlessly
around the divine presence. . . .
Having been firmly established
in the enlightenment they have received
and sharing in the very life of the One Who Is,
they share generously with others,
teaching them by word
about his enlightenment and graces.

—*Niketas Stethatos*


## 94

Once a soul has been consumed
in the depths of God's love
and has tasted the sweet delight
of God's intellective graces,[11]
it can no longer bear to stay frozen
in its own former condition
but is impelled to rise ever higher to the heavens.
The higher it ascends through the Spirit,
and the deeper it sinks into the abyss of God,
the more it is consumed by the fire of longing
and searches out the immensity
of the even deeper mysteries of God,
strenuously trying to come into that blessed light,
where every intellect is caught up into ecstasy,

where the heart knows it can finally rest
from all its strivings
and find its rest in joy.

*—Niketas Stethatos*


## 95

The heart that is constantly guarded
and not allowed to receive the forms, images,
or thoughts of the dark and evil spirits
will give birth from within itself
to thoughts that are radiant with light.

*—Hesychios*


## 96

The mystical stage of perfection belongs to those
who have already passed through all the degrees
so as to come to the "measure of the stature
EPH. 4:13    of the pleroma of Christ."
It is characterized by the spirit's passing through
the sphere of all the lesser aerial spirits
and entering the ranks of the higher celestials,
drawing near to the original light

to search out the depths of God in the Spirit.

It engages us in the perfection

of our contemplative spiritual vision

of the principles of God's providence,

justice, and truth,

and in the unraveling of hidden mysteries, symbols,

and obscure passages in holy Scripture.

The ultimate goal is to be mystically initiated

and perfected in the secret mysteries of God

and to be filled with ineffable wisdom

through our communion with the Holy Spirit,

so that we become wise theologians

in the great church of God,

enlightening others with theological discourse.

Whoever attains this stage,

through profound and penitent humility,

becomes like a second Apostle Paul,

for such a one

is caught up into the third heaven of theology

and hears ineffable words that mere mortals

still caught up in sense perception

are not permitted to hear.                                     2 COR. 12:1–4

Such a person experiences ineffable blessings

that no eye can see, no ear can hear,                          1 COR. 2:9

and so becomes a true servant of God,

God's very mouth . . .

a companion of those other theologians

who share the company of the highest angelic powers,
the cherubim and the seraphim,
who exemplify the essence of wisdom
and spiritual gnosis.

—*Niketas Stethatos*

## 97

The Spirit is light, life, and peace.
If you are illuminated by the divine Spirit,
your life will be established in peaceful serenity.
A spring will gush out within you,
which is the wisdom of the Logos
and the mystical knowledge of existent being,

I Cor. 2:16 and you will come to have the mind of Christ.
Then you will know the mysteries

Luke 8:10 of the Kingdom of God
and will enter the depths of the deity,
day by day speaking words of life for others
from a heart that is calmed and enlightened.

—*Niketas Stethatos*

## 98

The Logos does not take all his disciples and servants
along with him into the revelation

of his greater and more secret mysteries,
only those who have been given ears to hear,
whose eyes have been opened to see,
and whose tongues have been refashioned to speak clearly.
He takes these disciples,
separate from all the others—
even though these too are his disciples—
and he leads them up the mountain of Thabor,
which is the mountain of contemplation,
and there he is transfigured before them.                    Mark 9:1–8

—*Niketas Stethatos*

# 99

Lift up the eyes of your mind
to the light of the Gospel of Transfiguration,                Mark 9:1–8
so that you yourself might be transfigured
as your spiritual intellect is made new.
If this happens,
you will draw down the divine rays from on high
and will be conformed to the image
of the glory of the Lord,
whose face shone on the mountain
as radiant as the sun.

—*Gregory Palamas*

## 100

Come, true light.

Come, eternal life.

Come, hidden mystery.

Come, nameless treasure.

Come, Ineffable One.

Come, Inconceivable One.

Come, endless rejoicing.

Come, sun that never sets.

Come, true hope of all who wish to be saved.

Come, awakening of all who sleep.

Come, resurrection of the dead.

Come, Powerful One who ever creates and re-creates
and transfigures by your simple will.

Come, Invisible One beyond all touch or grasping.

Come, eternally Motionless One, ever active
to come to us and save us who lie in hell.

Come, beloved name repeated everywhere,
whose existence and nature we cannot express or know.

Come, eternal joy.

Come, untarnished crown.

Come, royal purple of our great King and God.

Come, jeweled belt of shining crystal.

Come, unapproachable sandal.

Come, imperial vestment.

Come, sovereign right hand.

Come, Lord,

whom my miserable soul has longed for
and longs for still.
Come, Solitary One, to this solitary,
for as you see, I am all alone. . . .
Come, for you have alienated me from all things
and made me be alone in this world.
Come, you who have become my desire
and have made me desire you, the Inaccessible One.
Come, my breath, my life.
Come, consolation of my poor soul.
Come, my joy, my glory, my endless delight.
For I must give you all my thanks
for making yourself one with me in spirit.

—*Symeon the New Theologian*

# AUTHORS AND TEXTS

*The numbers following the authors' names indicate the locations of their words in the text.*

## Aphrahat the Persian (1.8–11, 1.45)

Aphrahat lived in the early fourth century of the Christian era and was the first of the series of "Syriac fathers." He held some high office in the church (probably an early bishop) and composed a series of instructions on prayer and other matters called his *Demonstrations on Prayer*. He was one of the early ascetics among the Syrian Christians before monasticism became widely popular and organized.

## Apophthegmata Patrum (Sayings of the Fathers) (1.4, 1.46, 1.61–62, 2.23)

The sayings of the Egyptian desert fathers were collected by their disciples and other admirers and publicized from the late fourth century for an international Christian audience. One form was the brief "life and legend" of the holy person, but a common genre was a collection of their essential wisdom into short pithy sayings, or "apophthegms." Many of them were collected into alphabetical arrangement associated with the names of the various teachers. Often this is the only information that remains about individual historical characters.

## DIADOCHOS OF PHOTIKE (2.6–7, 2.9, 3.20–24)

Diadochos lived in the mid-fifth century of the Christian era and was bishop of Photike in Epirus, northern Greece. He was very interested in the developing monastic movement and composed treatises on prayer related to it, especially trying to moderate excessive trends he felt it was prone to. He is one of the first writers to speak about the Jesus Prayer as a way of focusing the intellect on short repeated invocations of the divine name. He exercised a great generic influence on his many successors.

## DOROTHEOS OF GAZA (2.5)

Dorotheos was a Syrian by origin who came to Egypt to study with famous ascetic elders. He was a student of Barsanuphius and John and founded his own monastery at Gaza circa 540. He had the foresight to see that the glory days of Christian monasticism in Egypt were coming to an end and tried to describe and collect the old oral tradition of the ancients into prose form. His series of "instructions" became standard material for training Eastern monks, and in the process he disseminated the Egyptian teachings widely in the Greek world. His system stresses the primacy of love and humility for spiritual advancement.

## EVAGRIOS OF PONTUS
### (1.22–44, 1.81, 2.21–22, 2.24–49, 3.27–31)

Evagrios (ca. 346–399) was a native of the Black Sea town of Ibora in Pontus. He was a disciple of the leading Cappadocian theologians of his day, and as a child he was taught rhetoric by Gregory of Nazianzus. His scintillating career as a Christian thinker and public speaker in Constantinople was cut short by a scandal and he fled for safety to Palestine. There he was advised by the famous ascetics Melania and Rufinus. Changing his life-style to a more ascetic form, he became a monk in Egypt and soon became known as the most famous of all the monastic teachers. His interests ranged across a wide spectrum of meta-physics, psychology, and mysticism. His doctrine was later chal-lenged, after his lifetime, and he was condemned by an imperial synod in the sixth century, but even with this posthumous set-back, his works ever afterward dominated the later Christian mystical tradition.

## GREGORY OF NAZIANZUS (2.14, 2.99)

Gregory, known as "the Theologian" in Byzantine Christianity, was a very wealthy man, the son of a bishop, and a close associate of the leading theologians of Cappadocia (Turkey) in the fourth century. He was the most educated Christian leader of his gen-eration and wrote extensive treatises, letters, poems, and ser-mons. He was copied almost as many times after his lifetime as was the Bible, and so became the most influential of all the Greek theologians. He was president of the international ecu-menical council held at Constantinople in 381, which defined the Christian doctrine of the trinity and was a major architect of that theology. His spiritual teaching lays great stress on the need for the soul's purification in light.

## GREGORY PALAMAS (3.99)

Gregory (ca. 1296–1359) was a Greek nobleman who, around 1318, became a monk on Mount Athos, the monastic complex near Thessalonica. He was chosen by the communities of Athos to defend their theological position, that it was possible to expe-rience the presence of God directly in a dedicated life of prayer and mysticism, against rationalist philosophical opponents heav-ily influenced by Western thirteenth-century empiricism. The resultant theological system he elaborated (known as Hesychasm, from the ancient concept of *hesychia*, or quietness of soul) became one of the most influential traditions of later Eastern Orthodox Christianity. It stresses the approach to God in luminous vision and the deifying transfiguration of material reality by the grace of the incarnate divinity present in Christ.

## HESYCHIOS (1.1, 2.4, 3.2–4, 3.32–35, 3.95)

Little is known of Hesychios apart from the fact that he composed books of "centuries" of sayings related to ascetic advice. He was probably an archimandrite (leader of a monastery) in Sinai sometime in the sixth or seventh century.

## IRENAEUS OF LYONS (3.9)

Irenaeus (ca. 130–200) was one of the most important of the early Christian bishops who fought against the Christian gnostic movement, which he felt endangered Christianity by transmuting a historically grounded revelation of God in Christ to the status of a nonmaterial symbol. He gave to Christianity its strong emphasis on ordered systems of governance and orthodox scriptures. Many of his early theological statements became standards of orthodoxy for later Christian thought. He has a broad cosmic vision of God's redemptive involvement in the world, which comes out in his spiritual remarks.

## ISAAC OF NINEVEH (3.8)

Isaac was a monk in Kurdistan sometime around 676. He eventually became bishop of Nineveh, but he preferred a more secluded life. He lived in solitude until he became blind as an old man and then returned to a community of monks who looked after him. He wrote extensive sermons advising his monastic followers. In the ninth century these were translated into Greek and exercised a great influence on Byzantine spiritual thought. Isaac lays special emphasis on the movement of the heart to the vision of God as the core value and focus of a spiritual life. He died sometime around 700.

## John of Apamea (1.13, 1.20)

Very little is known about the identity of John of Apamea, although he was certainly active in the early fifth century. He is also known as John the Solitary but has often been confused with another Palestinian writer named John of Lycopolis. John's chief work was his *Dialogue on the Soul*, and he also wrote other letters and small treatises. He enjoyed a great reputation as a spiritual master while alive, and his works have a directness and freshness that is greatly appealing.

## John Cassian (1.16–18)

John lived between 360 and sometime after 430. He was a Romanian (Scythian) by birth and left as a young man to join a monastery at Bethlehem, then moved to Egypt, where he was much influenced by the thought of Evagrios of Pontus. He became a deacon in Constantinople and was sent by John Chrysostom, the archbishop, on a diplomatic mission to the West. He remained in the West for the remainder of his life, founding a monastery at Marseilles, which became one of the great centers of ascetic life in the Latin world. His two greatest works were the *Institutes* and the *Conferences*, which became standard reference works for Benedictine monks after him. In them he brought Evagrios's doctrine, in a moderated form, to a much wider audience.

## John of Dalyutha (1.19, 3.7)

John is also known as John the Elder or John Sabaites. He was a native of Iraq and for many years was a mountain hermit, known for his austere lifestyle. His doctrine was circulated among a dedicated band of disciples. He fell into disfavor with local bishops for aspects of his doctrinal teaching, but his reputation as a master of the spiritual life was never diminished by any of the controversy. He was active in the eighth century.

## JOHN OF DAMASCUS (3.15)

John (ca. 655–750) was a high-ranking politician who was the Caliph's main minister of state for relations with the conquered Christian population of Damascus. He retired from political life and took refuge from intrigues in the Palestinian monastery of Saint Saba, near Bethlehem. Here he became known as a great hymn writer and systematic theologian. He was involved in the Byzantine controversy over images (iconoclasm) and wrote works defending the validity of venerating (though not worshiping) images of Christ and the saints, as important media of prayer. He composed many reference works on theology that had a lasting influence.

## JOHN OF KARPATHOS (2.12–13, 3.25–26)

John is more or less totally unknown apart from his short treatise written to advise the monks of "India"—this probably meant the monks of the highlands of Ethiopia who had asked for words of advice in times of troubles. It is presumed he was a native of the Greek island of Karpathos in the Sporades Islands. Even the century in which he wrote is not known.

## JOHN KLIMAKOS (1.7, 1.47–60, 1.82, 2.78)

John, the abbot of the monastery at Sinai, is known as Klimakos ("the ladder") from the title of his most famous work. He lived circa 570–649. He was for many years a solitary, loosely attached to the Sinai monastery, and at the end of a long life spent in solitude he returned to the monastery to serve as its leader. In this capacity he composed his *Ladder of Divine Ascent* as a manual of instruction for monks. It is still the most influential treatise on the monastic life in the Eastern church and is read as a basic preparatory text by novices to this day.

## Makarios the Great (1.14, 1.83–85, 2.8, 3.36–72)

Makarios the Great is an anonymous Syrian master of the spiritual life. His works attracted some controversy in his lifetime and were opposed by writers such as Diadochos of Photike. As a result, his name has been forgotten and the works themselves were somehow "fathered" pseudepigraphically onto another writer—the famous Macarius of Egypt, who had, in fact, left no written texts behind him. This was a common way the early Christians had of recycling material that had been officially censured if it struck them as of continuing importance. Makarios was active in the late fourth and fifth centuries in the border regions between Cappadocia (Turkey) and Syria. He stressed in his teachings the need for a "felt experience" of God in the spiritual life, and his works enjoyed a great vogue in their own time and again in the medieval period in Constantinople, where they exercised a formative influence over Hesychasm.

## Mark the Ascetic (1.12, 1.15)

Very little is known about the life of Mark the Ascetic. He is known also as Mark the Monk or Mark the Hermit. He is probably of the late fifth or early sixth century. He was certainly a hermit, in the monastic communes of either Egypt or Palestine. His work lays great stress on the futility of relying on personal merits in the quest for God and advocates a reliance on mercy and gracefulness—while attempting to do one's best—with great hope in God.

## Maximus the Confessor (1.71–80, 2.53–77, 2.79–81)

Maximus (ca. 580–662) is known as the Confessor because of the tradition that he was tortured by the Byzantine emperor because of his dissident writings in theology. He is one of the most important mystics and philosophers of the Byzantine era. He was an aristocrat in the court at Constantinople before becoming a monk. He traveled widely in the Greek and Latin world, and his writings were prolific. He lays great stress on a mystical vision of the cosmos permeated by the presence of God and focused in the grace of Christ. He sees this grace of redemption and transformation as constantly working to bring back "equilibrium" to an unbalanced world.

## Narsai of Edessa (3.5–6)

Narsai is also known as Narses. Born around 399, he died sometime in the early years of the sixth century. He was one of the most important east Syrian teachers of the fifth century, probably head of the church school (or university) at Edessa.

## Nicholas Cabasilas (3.73–75)

Nicholas Cabasilas (b. 1322) was the nephew of Nilus, the archbishop of Thessalonica, and one of the active members of the Hesychast school of spirituality. He wrote an influential explanation of the liturgical rites of the church, laying stress on their symbolic meanings, and also treatises on the spiritual life in which he emphasizes the hope of luminous transfiguration. It is thought that he became a monk late in life.

## Niketas Stethatos (2.1–2, 3.1, 3.88–94, 3.96–98)

Niketas was born around the beginning of the eleventh century and became a monk at the famous Studium monastery at Constantinople. He had some knowledge of Symeon the New Theologian, the most rhapsodic mystic of his age, and, after the death of Symeon, composed his biography and was partly responsible for the dissemination of his teachings on the vision of divine light and the transfiguring mercy of God. Later in life, as abbot of the Studite monastery, Niketas was one of those involved in controversy with the papacy and witnessed the great schism that occurred between the Latin and Greek churches in 1054. His spiritual doctrine is consistently insightful and optimistic in character.

## ORIGEN OF ALEXANDRIA (2.3)

Origen (ca. 185–254) was the most important philosopher-theologian of the early church, probably its most creative mind after the generation of the apostles. He laid down basic architectural structures in Christianity that have hardly been altered in their main outline since his day, such as an understanding of the Scriptures as canonical and the necessity of composing "commentaries" on them. His own writings are filled with a mystical desire to ascend in the soul to a restored union with the divine principle of the cosmos (the Logos). He sees the tragedy of the world as a fall from this primeval destiny of the human race.

## ABBA PHILEMON OF EGYPT (1.5–6, 1.21)

Philemon was a priest who lived an ascetic life in Egypt sometime during the Roman period, which suggests the late sixth or the seventh century. Nothing else is known of him. He wrote an influential *Discourse* about spiritual attentiveness. He is known as one of the important advocates of the Jesus Prayer, the frequently repeated phrase "Lord Jesus Christ, have mercy on me," which became a standard prayer form, and focus of meditation, of the Eastern church.

## SAHDONA THE SYRIAN (2.15–20)

Sahdona the Syrian is also known (in Greek) as Abba Martyrius. He was a seventh-century spiritual writer, a native Persian who became a monk, and eventually served as bishop of Mahoze in the Chaldean church. He was involved in controversies because of his theology and retired to an ascetic life at Edessa, where he wrote his chief work, *The Book of Perfection*, which is regarded as a masterpiece of world literature as well as being among the most important spiritual writings of the Syrian church.

### SAYINGS OF THE EGYPTIAN FATHERS (1.65–70)

The *Sayings of the Egyptian Fathers* is an edition of the monastic wisdom sayings collated from a variety of Egyptian teachers. Some sayings are listed alphabetically by the names of the writers; others are in more random collections. The collections show a lively oral tradition of spirituality in the desert monasteries. Most are directed at the training of monks in the early stages of ascetic life.

### SAYINGS OF THE ELDERS (1.2–3, 1.63–64)

The *Sayings of the Elders* is a Latin collection of the Egyptian wisdom sayings (apophthegmata); it had a wide dissemination and influenced much later Latin monastic thought as a standard book of recommended reading throughout the Middle Ages.

### SYMEON THE NEW THEOLOGIAN
### (1.86–87, 2.10–11, 2.82–83, 3.76–87, 3.100)

Symeon (949–1022) is one of the greatest mystic-poets of world literature. He was an aristocrat who became a monk in Constantinople and was head of a small monastery there, for which he wrote extensive treatises (*Catecheses*) outlining the elements of the ascetic life. He experienced hostility from the imperial court and was deposed as abbot in 1005 and sent into exile in 1009. His disciples accompanied him and founded a new monastery under his leadership. He wrote in exile some of the most rhapsodic of all Greek mystical poetry (*Hymns of Divine Love*). His doctrine laid great stress on the necessity for a real and personal experience of God and the need for affective passion in the search for God. He spoke about his own visions of the Divine in the form of radiant light. Symeon's later follower, Niketas Stethatos, wrote Symeon's biography and arranged to have his relics brought back to Constantinople thirty years after his death.

## THALASSIOS THE LIBYAN (2.84–98, 2.100, 3.10–14)

Thalassios (late sixth and early seventh centuries) was a contemporary and friend of Maximus the Confessor, who dedicated one of his major works to Thalassios and called himself his disciple. He was a priest and an archimandrite, the leader of a monastery, in Libya. His main works are in the form of "centuries" of advice on the spiritual life. He shows reliance on Evagrios, but his teaching, like that of Maximus, lays greater stress on the need for a more balanced harmony between body and soul in the spiritual quest.

## THEODOROS THE ASCETIC (1.88–96, 1.98–100, 2.50–52)

Very little is known about the life of Theodoros, except that he was a monk of Saint Saba monastery in Palestine (near Bethlehem) and eventually became the bishop of the Church of Edessa in Syria. He probably lived in the mid-seventh century (although some see him as a ninth-century writer). His "centuries" draw largely on the writings of Evagrios and Maximus.

## THEOGNOSTOS THE PRIEST (3.16–19)

The spiritual writer Theognostos is largely unknown, but his great interest in the priesthood and the sacraments show that he was certainly a priest himself. He quotes writers of the eighth century and therefore must be later than that period himself. His writing is vivid and cheerful, and he has a lively interest in the higher states of mystical consciousness.

# SOURCES

*In the sources provided below, the following abbreviations are used:*

DORRIES  Hermann Dorries, Erich Klostermann, and Mathias Kroeger, eds., *Die 50 Geistlichen Homilien des Makarios* (Berlin: DeGruyter, 1964).

DRISCOLL  Jeremy Driscoll, ed., *The Ad Monachos of Evagrius Ponticus* (Rome: Studia Anselmiana, 1991).

DE HALLEUX  André de Halleux, ed., *Martyrius (Sahdona) Oeuvres Spirituelles* (4 vols.), vol. 2, *The Book of Perfection* (Louvain, Belgium: Brepols, 1961).

JAEGER  Werner Jaeger, ed., *Two Rediscovered Works of Ancient Christian Literature: Gregory of Nyssa and Macarius* (Leiden, Netherlands: Brill, 1954). Pages 231–301 contain the text of Makarios's *Epistula Magna* (*The Great Letter*).

KODER  Johannes Koder, ed., *Saint Syméon le Nouveau Théologien: Les Hymnes de l'Amour Divin* (Paris: Sources Chrétiennes; vol. 51, 1957; vol. 96, 1973; vol. 156, 1969; vol. 174, 1971).

LAVENANT  René Lavenant, ed., *Oeuvres Spirituelles de S. Jean D'Apamée*, vol. 311 of *Sources Chrétiennes* (Paris: Sources Chrétiennes, 1984).

LXX  The Septuagint (ancient Greek translation of the Hebrew Scriptures used by the early Christians).

MILLER   David Miller, ed. and trans., *The Ascetical Homilies of St. Isaac the Syrian* (Boston: Holy Transfiguration Monastery, 1984).

PG   Jacques Paul Migne, ed., *Cursus Completus Patrologiae*, Series Graeca, 161 vols. (Paris: Éditions Garnier, 1857–1866).

PHILOKALIA   *Philokalia Ton Ieron Niptikon Syneranistheisa Para Ton Agion Kai Theophoron Pateron Imon*, 5 vols. (Athens: Astir Publishing, 1957–1963).

PL   Jacques Paul Migne, ed., *Cursus Completus Patrologiae*, Series Latina, 221 vols. (Paris: Éditions Garnier, 1844–1864).

PO   *Patrologia Orientalis*, ed. Richard Griffin and François Nau (Paris, 1897; Turnhout, Belgium: Brepols, 1904– ), vol. 39, part 3, *La Collection des Lettres de Jean de Dalyatha*, ed. Robert Beulay (Turnhout, Belgium: Brepols, 1978).

PS   Jean Parisot, ed., *Patrologia Syriaca*, vol. 1, part 1, *Aphrahat the Persian: Demonstration Four on Prayer* (Paris, Éditions Firmin-Didot, 1894).

SC   *Sources Chrétiennes* (Paris: Sources Chrétiennes, 1942– ). A collection of critical editions of ancient Christian literature published by Sources Chrétiennes, with French translations; more than three hundred volumes to date.

SIMAN   Emmanuel Pataq Siman, ed., *Narsai: Cinq homélies sur les paraboles évangéliques* (Paris: Cariscript, 1984).

# Praktikos

1.1   Hesychios, *On Watchfulness* 122. *Philokalia* 1:159–60.

1.2   *Sayings of the Elders.* PL 73:856.

1.3   *Sayings of the Elders.* PL 73:858.

1.4   *Apophthegmata Patrum*, Amma Sarra. PG 65:420.

1.5   Abba Philemon, *The Discourse. Philokalia* 2:242.

1.6   Abba Philemon, *The Discourse. Philokalia* 2:242.

1.7 John Klimakos, *The Ladder* 7.64. PG 88:804.

1.8 Aphrahat the Persian, *Demonstration on Prayer* 4.10. PS 1:157–60.

1.9 Aphrahat the Persian, *Demonstration on Prayer* 4.13. PS 1:165–66.

1.10 Aphrahat the Persian, *Demonstration on Prayer* 4.13. PS 1:169–70.

1.11 Aphrahat the Persian, *Demonstration on Prayer* 4.13. PS 1.165–66.

1.12 Mark the Ascetic, *On Those Who Presume They Can Negotiate Their Salvation* 74. *Philokalia* 1:114.

1.13 John of Apamea, *Second Dialogue with Thomasios*. Lavenant, SC 311:61.

1.14 Makarios the Great, *Fifty Spiritual Homilies* 43.3. Dorries, 286.

1.15 Mark the Ascetic, *On Those Who Presume They Can Negotiate Their Salvation* 34. *Philokalia* 1:110.

1.16 John Cassian, *On the Eight Vices*. *Philokalia* 1:72.

1.17 John Cassian, *On the Eight Vices*. *Philokalia* 1:71–72.

1.18 John Cassian, *On the Eight Vices*. *Philokalia* 1:80.

1.19 John of Dalyutha, Letter 28.2. PO 39.3:388–89.

1.20 John of Apamea, *First Dialogue with Thomasios* 8. Lavenant, SC 311:53–54.

1.21 Abba Philemon, *The Discourse*. *Philokalia* 2:244.

1.22 Evagrios of Pontus, *Chapters on Prayer* 2. *Philokalia* 1:177.

1.23 Evagrios of Pontus, *Chapters on Prayer* 11. *Philokalia* 1:178.

1.24 Evagrios of Pontus, *Chapters on Prayer* 22. *Philokalia* 1:178.

1.25 Evagrios of Pontus, *Chapters on Prayer* 27. *Philokalia* 1:179.

1.26 Evagrios of Pontus, *Chapters on Prayer* 29. *Philokalia* 1:179.

1.27    Evagrios of Pontus, *Chapters on Prayer* 31. *Philokalia* 1:179.

1.28    Evagrios of Pontus, *Chapters on Prayer* 32. *Philokalia* 1:179.

1.29    Evagrios of Pontus, *Chapters on Prayer* 42. *Philokalia* 1:180.

1.30    Evagrios of Pontus, *Chapters on Prayer* 45. *Philokalia* 1:180.

1.31    Evagrios of Pontus, *Chapters on Prayer* 47. *Philokalia* 1:180.

1.32    Evagrios of Pontus, *Chapters on Prayer* 54. *Philokalia* 1:181.

1.33    Evagrios of Pontus, *Chapters on Prayer* 62. *Philokalia* 1:182.

1.34    Evagrios of Pontus, *Chapters on Prayer* 72. *Philokalia* 1:183.

1.35    Evagrios of Pontus, *Chapters on Prayer* 81. *Philokalia* 1:184.

1.36    Evagrios of Pontus, *Chapters on Prayer* 92, 94, 114. *Philokalia* 1:184–85, 187.

1.37    Evagrios of Pontus, *Chapters on Prayer* 101. *Philokalia* 1:185.

1.38    Evagrios of Pontus, *Chapters on Prayer* 131. *Philokalia* 1:187.

1.39    Evagrios of Pontus, *Chapters on Prayer* 145. *Philokalia* 1:189.

1.40    Evagrios of Pontus, *Chapters on Prayer* 146. *Philokalia* 1:189.

1.41    Evagrios of Pontus, *Chapters on Prayer* 147. *Philokalia* 1:189.

1.42    Evagrios of Pontus, *Chapters on Prayer* 149. *Philokalia* 1:189.

1.43    Evagrios of Pontus, *Texts on Watchfulness* 5 (cf. *Praktikos* 15). *Philokalia* 1:58.

1.44   Evagrios of Pontus, *Address to the Monks* 117. Driscoll
       (appendix).
1.45   Aphrahat the Persian, *Demonstration on Prayer* 4.16.
       PS 1:173–74.
1.46   *Apophthegmata Patrum*, Amma Syncletica 3. PG 65:421.
1.47   John Klimakos, *The Ladder* 5.30. PG 88:777.
1.48   John Klimakos, *The Ladder* 9.10. PG 88:841.
1.49   John Klimakos, *The Ladder* 19.5. PG 88:937.
1.50   John Klimakos, *The Ladder* 19.8. PG 88:937.
1.51   John Klimakos, *The Ladder* 23.12. PG 88:968.
1.52   John Klimakos, *The Ladder* 26.38. PG 88:1088.
1.53   John Klimakos, *The Ladder* 26.54. PG 88:1089.
1.54   John Klimakos, *The Ladder* 27.61. PG 88:1112.
1.55   John Klimakos, *The Ladder* 27.77. PG 88:1116.
1.56   John Klimakos, *The Ladder* 27.81. PG 88:1116.
1.57   John Klimakos, *The Ladder* 28.4. PG 88:1129.
1.58   John Klimakos, *The Ladder* 28.5. PG 88:1129.
1.59   John Klimakos, *The Ladder* 28.11. PG 88:1132.
1.60   John Klimakos, *The Ladder* 28.44. PG 88:1137.
1.61   *Apophthegmata Patrum*, Abba Agathon. PG 65:112.
1.62   *Apophthegmata Patrum*, Abba Agathon. PG 65:109.
1.63   *Sayings of the Elders*. PL 73:1032.
1.64   *Sayings of the Elders*. PL 73:1034.
1.65   *Sayings of the Egyptian Fathers* 46. PL 74:389.
1.66   *Sayings of the Egyptian Fathers* 64. PL 74:390.
1.67   *Sayings of the Egyptian Fathers* 72. PL 74:391.
1.68   *Sayings of the Egyptian Fathers* 76–77. PL 74:391.
1.69   *Sayings of the Egyptian Fathers* 83. PL 74:391.
1.70   *Sayings of the Egyptian Fathers* 109. PL 74:394.
1.71   Maximus the Confessor, *Centuries on Charity* 1.1.
       *Philokalia* 2:4.
1.72   Maximus the Confessor, *Centuries on Charity* 1.3.
       *Philokalia* 2:4.
1.73   Maximus the Confessor, *Centuries on Charity* 1.14.
       *Philokalia* 2:5.

1.74 Maximus the Confessor, *Centuries on Charity* 1.15. *Philokalia* 2:5.

1.75 Maximus the Confessor, *Centuries on Charity* 1.23. *Philokalia* 2:5.

1.76 Maximus the Confessor, *Centuries on Charity* 1.24. *Philokalia* 2:5.

1.77 Maximus the Confessor, *Centuries on Charity* 1.45. *Philokalia* 2:7.

1.78 Maximus the Confessor, *Centuries on Charity* 1.58. *Philokalia* 2:9.

1.79 Maximus the Confessor, *Centuries on Charity* 1.85. *Philokalia* 2:12.

1.80 Maximus the Confessor, *Centuries on Charity* 1.89. *Philokalia* 2:12.

1.81 Evagrios of Pontus, *Chapters on Prayer* 61. *Philokalia* 1:182.

1.82 John Klimakos, *The Ladder* 7.15. PG 88:805.

1.83 Makarios the Great, *Fifty Spiritual Homilies* 43.7. Dorries, 289.

1.84 Makarios the Great, *Fifty Spiritual Homilies* 43.2. Dorries, 283–84.

1.85 Makarios the Great, *Fifty Spiritual Homilies* 43.2. Dorries, 285.

1.86 Symeon the New Theologian, *Practical and Gnostic Chapters* 1.71. Koder, SC, 51.

1.87 Symeon the New Theologian, *On the Three Methods of Prayer*. *Philokalia* 5:87–88.

1.88 Theodoros the Ascetic, *Spiritual Chapters* 8. *Philokalia* 1:305.

1.89 Theodoros the Ascetic, *Spiritual Chapters* 9. *Philokalia* 1:305.

1.90 Theodoros the Ascetic, *Spiritual Chapters* 17. *Philokalia* 1:307.

1.91 Theodoros the Ascetic, *Spiritual Chapters* 27. *Philokalia* 1:308.

## Theoretikos

2.9    Diadochos of Photike, *On Spiritual Knowledge* 67.
       *Philokalia* 1:255.

2.10   Symeon the New Theologian, *On the Three Methods of
       Prayer. Philokalia* 5:84–85.

2.11   Symeon the New Theologian, *On the Three Methods of
       Prayer. Philokalia* 5:84–85.

2.12   John of Karpathos, *To the Monks of India* 70. *Philokalia*
       1:291.

2.13   John of Karpathos, *To the Monks of India* 71. *Philokalia*
       1:291.

2.14   Gregory of Nazianzus, *Oration* 27.4. PG 36:16.

2.15   Sahdona the Syrian, *The Book of Perfection*, part 2, 4.7.
       De Halleux 2:33.

2.16   Sahdona the Syrian, *The Book of Perfection*, part 2, 4.9.
       De Halleux 2:34.

2.17   Sahdona the Syrian, *The Book of Perfection*, part 2, 4.7.
       De Halleux 2:33.

2.18   Sahdona the Syrian, *The Book of Perfection*, part 2, 4.14.
       De Halleux 2:36.

2.19   Sahdona the Syrian, *The Book of Perfection*, part 2, 4.11.
       De Halleux 2:35.

2.20   Sahdona the Syrian, *The Book of Perfection*, part 2, 4.33.
       De Halleux 2:43.

2.21   Evagrios of Pontus, *Chapters on Prayer* 71. *Philokalia*
       1:182.

2.22   Evagrios of Pontus, *Address to the Monks* 120. Driscoll
       (appendix).

2.23   *Apophthegmata Patrum*, Abba Antony. PG 65:85.

2.24   Evagrios of Pontus, *Praktikos* 2. PG 40:1221.

2.25   Evagrios of Pontus, *Praktikos* 3. PG 40:1221.

2.26   Evagrios of Pontus, *Praktikos* 21 (renumbered as 32 in
       SC, vols. 170–71); PG 40:1228.

2.27   Evagrios of Pontus, *Praktikos* 36 (renumbered as 64 in
       SC, vols. 170–71); PG 40:1232.

2.28   Evagrios of Pontus, *Praktikos* 38 (renumbered as 66 in SC, vols. 170–71); PG 40:1232.

2.29   Evagrios of Pontus, *Praktikos* 51 (renumbered as 79 in SC, vols. 170–71); PG 40:1233.

2.30   Evagrios of Pontus, *Praktikos* 53 (renumbered as 81 in SC, vols. 170–71); PG 40:1233.

2.31   Evagrios of Pontus, *Chapters on Prayer* 3. *Philokalia* 1:177.

2.32   Evagrios of Pontus, *Chapters on Prayer* 15. *Philokalia* 1:178.

2.33   Evagrios of Pontus, *Chapters on Prayer* 16. *Philokalia* 1:178.

2.34   Evagrios of Pontus, *Chapters on Prayer* 23. *Philokalia* 1:178.

2.35   Evagrios of Pontus, *Chapters on Prayer* 33a. *Philokalia* 1:179.

2.36   Evagrios of Pontus, *Chapters on Prayer* 33b. *Philokalia* 1:179.

2.37   Evagrios of Pontus, *Chapters on Prayer* 34a. *Philokalia* 1:179.

2.38   Evagrios of Pontus, *Chapters on Prayer* 34b. *Philokalia* 1:179.

2.39   Evagrios of Pontus, *Chapters on Prayer* 35. *Philokalia* 1:180.

2.40   Evagrios of Pontus, *Chapters on Prayer* 52. *Philokalia* 1:181.

2.41   Evagrios of Pontus, *Chapters on Prayer* 53. *Philokalia* 1:181.

2.42   Evagrios of Pontus, *Chapters on Prayer* 60. *Philokalia* 1:181.

2.43   Evagrios of Pontus, *On Discrimination*. *Philokalia* 1:54.

2.44   Evagrios of Pontus, *Chapters on Prayer* 67. *Philokalia* 1:182.

2.45   Evagrios of Pontus, *Chapters on Prayer* 76. *Philokalia* 1:183.

2.46     Evagrios of Pontus, *Chapters on Prayer* 77. *Philokalia* 1:183.

2.47     Evagrios of Pontus, *Chapters on Prayer* 80. *Philokalia* 1:183.

2.48     Evagrios of Pontus, *Chapters on Prayer* 150. *Philokalia* 1:189.

2.49     Evagrios of Pontus, *Chapters on Prayer* 153. *Philokalia* 1:189.

2.50     Theodoros the Ascetic, *Spiritual Chapters* 29. *Philokalia* 1:309.

2.51     Theodoros the Ascetic, *Spiritual Chapters* 88. *Philokalia* 1:320.

2.52     Theodoros the Ascetic, *Spiritual Chapters* 94. *Philokalia* 1:322.

2.53     Maximus the Confessor, *Centuries on Charity* 1.12. *Philokalia* 2:4–5.

2.54     Maximus the Confessor, *Centuries on Charity* 1.19. *Philokalia* 2:5.

2.55     Maximus the Confessor, *Centuries on Charity* 4.20. *Philokalia* 2:43.

2.56     Maximus the Confessor, *Centuries on Charity* 4.36. *Philokalia* 2:44.

2.57     Maximus the Confessor, *Centuries on Charity* 4.39. *Philokalia* 2:45.

2.58     Maximus the Confessor, *Centuries on Charity* 4.56. *Philokalia* 2:46.

2.59     Maximus the Confessor, *Centuries on Charity* 4.64. *Philokalia* 2:47.

2.60     Maximus the Confessor, *Centuries on Charity* 4.72. *Philokalia* 2:48.

2.61     Maximus the Confessor, *Centuries on Charity* 4.79. *Philokalia* 2:49.

2.62     Maximus the Confessor, *Centuries on Charity* 4.80. *Philokalia* 2:49.

2.63    Maximus the Confessor, *Centuries on Charity* 4.86.
        *Philokalia* 2:50.

2.64    Maximus the Confessor, *Centuries on Charity* 4.90.
        *Philokalia* 2:50.

2.65    Maximus the Confessor, *Centuries on Theology* 1.12.
        *Philokalia* 2:53.

2.66    Maximus the Confessor, *Centuries on Theology* 1.16.
        *Philokalia* 2:54.

2.67    Maximus the Confessor, *Centuries on Theology* 1.30.
        *Philokalia* 2:56.

2.68    Maximus the Confessor, *Centuries on Theology* 1.31.
        *Philokalia* 2:56.

2.69    Maximus the Confessor, *Centuries on Theology* 1.33.
        *Philokalia* 2:56.

2.70    Maximus the Confessor, *Centuries on Theology* 1.33.
        *Philokalia* 2:56–57.

2.71    Maximus the Confessor, *Centuries on Theology* 1.39.
        *Philokalia* 2:58.

2.72    Maximus the Confessor, *Centuries on Theology* 2.86.
        *Philokalia* 2:86.

2.73    Maximus the Confessor, *Centuries on Theology* 2.87.
        *Philokalia* 2:86–87.

2.74    Maximus the Confessor, *Centuries on Theology* 2.88.
        *Philokalia* 2:87.

2.75    Maximus the Confessor, *Centuries of Various Texts* 1.50.
        *Philokalia* 2:99.

2.76    Maximus the Confessor, *Centuries of Various Texts* 1.54.
        *Philokalia* 2:100.

2.77    Maximus the Confessor, *Centuries of Various Texts* 1.62.
        *Philokalia* 2:101–2.

2.78    John Klimakos, *The Ladder* 26.82. PG 88:1029.

2.79    Maximus the Confessor, *Centuries of Various Texts* 1.78.
        *Philokalia* 2:105.

2.80    Maximus the Confessor, *Centuries of Various Texts* 1.95.
        *Philokalia* 2:108.

2.81     Maximus the Confessor, *Centuries of Various Texts* 1.96. *Philokalia* 2:108.

2.82     Symeon the New Theologian, *On the Three Methods of Prayer. Philokalia* 5:86–87.

2.83     Symeon the New Theologian, *On the Three Methods of Prayer. Philokalia* 5:87.

2.84     Thalassios the Libyan, *Centuries on Love* 1.1. *Philokalia* 2:205.

2.85     Thalassios the Libyan, *Centuries on Love* 1.5. *Philokalia* 2:205.

2.86     Thalassios the Libyan, *Centuries on Love* 1.7. *Philokalia* 2:205.

2.87     Thalassios the Libyan, *Centuries on Love* 1.11. *Philokalia* 2:206.

2.88     Thalassios the Libyan, *Centuries on Love* 1.22. *Philokalia* 2:206.

2.89     Thalassios the Libyan, *Centuries on Love* 1.44. *Philokalia* 2:207.

2.90     Thalassios the Libyan, *Centuries on Love* 1.48. *Philokalia* 2:207.

2.91     Thalassios the Libyan, *Centuries on Love* 1.50. *Philokalia* 2:208.

2.92     Thalassios the Libyan, *Centuries on Love* 1.51. *Philokalia* 2:208.

2.93     Thalassios the Libyan, *Centuries on Love* 1.55. *Philokalia* 2:208.

2.94     Thalassios the Libyan, *Centuries on Love* 1.56. *Philokalia* 2:208.

2.95     Thalassios the Libyan, *Centuries on Love* 1.73. *Philokalia* 2:209.

2.96     Thalassios the Libyan, *Centuries on Love* 1.100. *Philokalia* 2:210.

2.97     Thalassios the Libyan, *Centuries on Love* 3.84. *Philokalia* 2:221.

2.98 Thalassios the Libyan, *Centuries on Love* 4.4. *Philokalia* 2:223.

2.99 Gregory of Nazianzus, *Oration* 40. PG 36:363.

2.100 Thalassios the Libyan, *Centuries on Love* 3.99–100. *Philokalia* 2:222.

# Gnostikos

3.1 Niketas Stethatos, *Gnostic Chapters* 41. *Philokalia* 3:335–36.

3.2 Hesychios, *On Watchfulness* 89. *Philokalia* 1:154.

3.3 Hesychios, *On Watchfulness* 104. *Philokalia* 1:157.

3.4 Hesychios, *On Watchfulness* 132. *Philokalia* 1:161.

3.5 Narsai of Edessa, *The Parable of Dives and Lazarus* 241. Siman, 58.

3.6 Narsai of Edessa, *The Parable of the Vineyard* 59–63. Siman, 65.

3.7 John of Dalyutha, Letter 28.2. PO 39.3:388–89.

3.8 Isaac of Nineveh, *The Ascetical Homilies* 35. Miller (adapted), 158.

3.9 Irenaeus of Lyons, *Against the Heresies* 4.20.5–6. PG 7:1035.

3.10 Thalassios the Libyan, *Centuries on Love* 4.66. *Philokalia* 2:226.

3.11 Thalassios the Libyan, *Centuries on Love* 4.73. *Philokalia* 2:227.

3.12 Thalassios the Libyan, *Centuries on Love* 4.75. *Philokalia* 2:227.

3.13 Thalassios the Libyan, *Centuries on Love* 4.78. *Philokalia* 2:227.

3.14 Thalassios the Libyan, *Centuries on Love* 4.81. *Philokalia* 2:227.

3.15 John of Damascus, *Discourse on the Transfiguration* 10. PG 96:561.

3.16    Theognostos the Priest, *On the Practice of the Virtues* ("On Priesthood," in English *Philokalia*) 10. *Philokalia* 2:257.

3.17    Theognostos the Priest, *On the Practice of the Virtues* ("On Priesthood," in English *Philokalia*) 12. *Philokalia* 2:257.

3.18    Theognostos the Priest, *On the Practice of the Virtues* ("On Priesthood," in English *Philokalia*) 69. *Philokalia* 2:269.

3.19    Theognostos the Priest, *On the Practice of the Virtues* ("On Priesthood," in English *Philokalia*) 69. *Philokalia* 2:269.

3.20    Diadochos of Photike, *On Spiritual Knowledge* 7. *Philokalia* 1:237.

3.21    Diadochos of Photike, *On Spiritual Knowledge* 59. *Philokalia* 1:251.

3.22    Diadochos of Photike, *On Spiritual Knowledge* 14. *Philokalia* 1:238–39.

3.23    Diadochos of Photike, *On Spiritual Knowledge* 33. *Philokalia* 1:243–44.

3.24    Diadochos of Photike, *On Spiritual Knowledge* 69. *Philokalia* 1:255.

3.25    John of Karpathos, *To the Monks of India* 34. *Philokalia* 1:283.

3.26    John of Karpathos, *To the Monks of India* 98. *Philokalia* 1:296.

3.27    Evagrios of Pontus, *On Discrimination* 14. *Philokalia* 1:52.

3.28    Evagrios of Pontus, *On Discrimination* 17. *Philokalia* 1:54.

3.29    Evagrios of Pontus, *Chapters on Prayer* 113. *Philokalia* 1:187.

3.30    Evagrios of Pontus, *Chapters on Prayer* 142. *Philokalia* 1:188.

3.31   Evagrios of Pontus, *Address to the Monks* 3. Driscoll (appendix).

3.32   Hesychios, *On Watchfulness* 35. *Philokalia* 1:147.

3.33   Hesychios, *On Watchfulness* 156. *Philokalia* 1:165.

3.34   Hesychios, *On Watchfulness* 196. *Philokalia* 1:172.

3.35   Hesychios, *On Watchfulness* 197. *Philokalia* 1:172.

3.36   Makarios the Great, *Fifty Spiritual Homilies* 1.2. Dorries, 1–2.

3.37   Makarios the Great, *Fifty Spiritual Homilies* 1.2. Dorries, 2.

3.38   Makarios the Great, *Fifty Spiritual Homilies* 1.2. Dorries, 2.

3.39   Makarios the Great, *Fifty Spiritual Homilies* 1.4. Dorries, 5.

3.40   Makarios the Great, *Fifty Spiritual Homilies* 1.12. Dorries, 12.

3.41   Makarios the Great, *Fifty Spiritual Homilies* 2.5. Dorries, 18–19.

3.42   Makarios the Great, *Fifty Spiritual Homilies* 4.13. Dorries, 37.

3.43   Makarios the Great, *Fifty Spiritual Homilies* 4.16. Dorries, 39.

3.44   Makarios the Great, *Fifty Spiritual Homilies* 5.6. Dorries, 50.

3.45   Makarios the Great, *Fifty Spiritual Homilies* 5.10. Dorries, 61–62.

3.46   Makarios the Great, *Fifty Spiritual Homilies* 5.11. Dorries, 62.

3.47   Makarios the Great, *Fifty Spiritual Homilies* 8.2. Dorries, 78.

3.48   Makarios the Great, *Fifty Spiritual Homilies* 9.12. Dorries, 90.

3.49   Makarios the Great, *Fifty Spiritual Homilies* 10.4. Dorries, 95–96.

3.50   Makarios the Great, *Fifty Spiritual Homilies* 15.42.
       Dorries, 152.
3.51   Makarios the Great, *Fifty Spiritual Homilies* 16.7.
       Dorries, 162.
3.52   Makarios the Great, *Fifty Spiritual Homilies* 17.1.
       Dorries, 166.
3.53   Makarios the Great, *Fifty Spiritual Homilies* 18.2.
       Dorries, 177–78.
3.54   Makarios the Great, *Fifty Spiritual Homilies* 18.7.
       Dorries, 180.
3.55   Makarios the Great, *Fifty Spiritual Homilies* 18.9.
       Dorries, 181.
3.56   Makarios the Great, *Fifty Spiritual Homilies* 24.6.
       Dorries, 199.
3.57   Makarios the Great, *Fifty Spiritual Homilies* 29.1.
       Dorries, 235–36.
3.58   Makarios the Great, *Fifty Spiritual Homilies* 31.5.
       Dorries, 249–50.
3.59   Makarios the Great, *Fifty Spiritual Homilies* 33.2.
       Dorries, 258.
3.60   Makarios the Great, *Fifty Spiritual Homilies* 33.4.
       Dorries, 259–60.
3.61   Makarios the Great, *Fifty Spiritual Homilies* 34.1.
       Dorries, 260.
3.62   Makarios the Great, *Fifty Spiritual Homilies* 43.1.
       Dorries, 283.
3.63   Makarios the Great, *Fifty Spiritual Homilies* 44.5.
       Dorries, 293.
3.64   Makarios the Great, *Fifty Spiritual Homilies* 44.9.
       Dorries, 295.
3.65   Makarios the Great, *Fifty Spiritual Homilies* 45.6.
       Dorries, 300.
3.66   Makarios the Great, *Fifty Spiritual Homilies* 46.4.
       Dorries, 303.

3.67 Makarios the Great, *Fifty Spiritual Homilies* 46.6. Dorries, 304.

3.68 Makarios the Great, *Fifty Spiritual Homilies* 47.14. Dorries, 310.

3.69 Makarios the Great, *Fifty Spiritual Homilies* 47.17. Dorries, 311–12.

3.70 Makarios the Great, *The Great Letter.* Jaeger, 239.

3.71 Makarios the Great, *The Great Letter.* Jaeger, 241.

3.72 Makarios the Great, *The Great Letter.* Jaeger, 300.

3.73 Nicholas Cabasilas, *The Life in Christ* 4.19–20. PG 150:624.

3.74 Nicholas Cabasilas, *The Life in Christ* 4.20. PG 150:624.

3.75 Nicholas Cabasilas, *The Life in Christ* 1.6. PG 150:504.

3.76 Symeon the New Theologian, *Hymns of Divine Love* 1. Koder, SC 156:157–58.

3.77 Symeon the New Theologian, *Hymns of Divine Love* 1. Koder, SC 156:168.

3.78 Symeon the New Theologian, *Hymns of Divine Love* 2. Koder, SC 156:178.

3.79 Symeon the New Theologian, *Hymns of Divine Love* 3. Koder, SC 156:188.

3.80 Symeon the New Theologian, *Hymns of Divine Love* 11. Koder, SC 156:238.

3.81 Symeon the New Theologian, *Hymns of Divine Love* 17. Koder, SC 174:41.

3.82 Symeon the New Theologian, *Hymns of Divine Love* 24. Koder, SC 174:226–28.

3.83 Symeon the New Theologian, *Hymns of Divine Love* 27. Koder, SC 174:288.

3.84 Symeon the New Theologian, *Hymns of Divine Love* 30. Koder, SC 174:366–70.

3.85 Symeon the New Theologian, *Hymns of Divine Love* 34. Koder, SC 174:432–34.

3.86 Symeon the New Theologian, *Hymns of Divine Love* 37. Koder, SC 174:460.

3.87    Symeon the New Theologian, *Hymns of Divine Love* 47. Koder, SC 96:124.

3.88    Niketas Stethatos, *Gnostic Chapters* 1. *Philokalia* 3:326.

3.89    Niketas Stethatos, *Gnostic Chapters* 3. *Philokalia* 3:326.

3.90    Niketas Stethatos, *Gnostic Chapters* 12. *Philokalia* 3:329.

3.91    Niketas Stethatos, *Gnostic Chapters* 21. *Philokalia* 3:331.

3.92    Niketas Stethatos, *Gnostic Chapters* 23. *Philokalia* 3:331.

3.93    Niketas Stethatos, *Gnostic Chapters* 27. *Philokalia.* 3:332.

3.94    Niketas Stethatos, *Gnostic Chapters* 37. *Philokalia* 3:334.

3.95    Hesychios, *On Watchfulness* 104. *Philokalia* 1:157.

3.96    Niketas Stethatos, *Gnostic Chapters* 44. *Philokalia* 3:336–37.

3.97    Niketas Stethatos, *Gnostic Chapters* 46. *Philokalia* 3:337.

3.98    Niketas Stethatos, *Gnostic Chapters* 83. *Philokalia* 3:350.

3.99    Gregory Palamas, *Homily* 35. PG 151:437.

3.100   Symeon the New Theologian, *The Mystical Prayer.* Koder, SC 156:150–52.

# NOTES

1. *Spiritual intellect.* This is the most common English rendition of *nous*, a term Evagrios used constantly. This is literally the intelligence but means much more than our modern notion of intellect: for Evagrios and the ancient Christian, the term carried the weight of psychic awareness and was commonly seen as the place where the divine power had imaged itself most directly in the human creature. The *nous*, or spiritual intellect, was, therefore, the part most akin to the Godhead in a person's composite existence.

2. *Ideations.* Evagrios believed that given sufficient attention, our mind's thoughts rise to a new level, taking on a ghostly life of their own and obscuring the spiritual intellect.

3. *In the humanity.* This refers to the common patristic doctrine that Christ has two natures, divine and human—that is, that he is one person who acts both "in the humanity" (eating, weeping, dying, and so on) and in the divinity (rising from the dead, communing with the Father, and so forth).

4. *A theologian.* Cf. John 13:23–26: the disciple John, who rested on the breast of Jesus at the Last Supper, is known in Greek Christian tradition as John the Theologian.

5. *Pleroma.* Signifies the cosmic totality of a mystery. It alludes to Christ as the source of universal grace, as in Paul's Letter to the Ephesians. Maximus envisages the mystical union with Christ as an entry into the pleroma, comparable with what he says about divinization in the following passage.

6. *Divinized.* This is an important term in Greek Christian thought. It evokes the power of divine grace to transfigure the earthly nature into a graced nature, thus bringing it into communion with God and suffusing it with the divine presence in a manner analogous to the way the divine Logos assumed human nature (was made incarnate). This sentence boldly draws a parallel between the incarnation of God and the deification of the human race. As one of the early theologians put it: "God became man that man might be rendered divine."

7. *Adoption.* Irenaeus is alluding to the Pauline text (Rom. 8:15, Gal. 4:5, Eph. 1:5) that speaks of God's adopting sons (that is, the human race) through the work of his true Son, Jesus.

8. *Chrism.* The sacred oil used to anoint the kings and priest-prophets of ancient Israel. In the Christian church it is still used to anoint the person at baptism. It evokes the sacramental consecration of the newly baptized as prophet, priest, and king. Makarios is comparing the higher stages of mystical initiation to a new stage of baptismal initiation—a more perfect assimilation into the Christ.

9. *Charism.* From the New Testament Greek word *charismata.* It signifies the various graces that Christ gives to disciples so that the church as a community will always be enlivened and energized with a diversity of communal gifts.

10. *Paraclete.* The title given by Jesus to the spirit of God, considered as "advocate" or "comforter." See, for example, John 14:16 and 26.

11. *God's intellective graces.* Niketas means this in the particular sense of God's activity in the higher level of the human spirit. The presence of God within the soul in this way is signaled by the special grace of God that sweeps the soul into rapture and fills it with longing for greater immersion in the divine presence.

# BIBLIOGRAPHY

## Primary Texts

Bamberger, John E., trans. *Evagrius Ponticus: Praktikos and Chapters on Prayer.* Cistercian Studies Series, no. 4. Kalamazoo, Mich.: Cistercian Publications, 1972. Reprint, 1989.

Brock, Sebastian, trans. *The Syriac Fathers on Prayer and the Spiritual Life.* Kalamazoo, Mich.: Cistercian Publications, 1987.

Gendle, Nicholas, trans. *Gregory Palamas: The Triads.* New York: Paulist Press, 1983.

Maloney, George A., trans. *Symeon the New Theologian: Hymns of Divine Love.* Denville, N.J.: n.p., n.d. [1975; reprint, 1998].

———. *Pseudo-Macarius: The Fifty Spiritual Homilies and the Great Letter.* New York: Paulist Press, 1992.

McGuckin, Paul [John Anthony]. *Symeon the New Theologian: The Practical and Theological Chapters.* Kalamazoo, Mich.: Cistercian Publications, 1982. Reprint, 1994.

Moore, Lazarus, trans. *John Climacus: The Ladder of Divine Ascent.* London: Mowbrays, 1959. Reprint, Boston: Holy Transfiguration Monastery, 1991.

Palmer, Gerard E., Philip Sherrard, and Kallistos Ware, eds. and trans. *The Philokalia.* 5 vols. London: Faber and Faber, 1979. Vol. 1, 1979, includes works of Evagrios, Hesychios,

Diadochos, John of Karpathos; vol. 2, 1981, includes Maximus the Confessor, Theodoros, Thalassios, Theognostos; vol. 4, 1995, includes Niketas Stethatos, Symeon the New Theologian, Gregory Palamas.

Stewart, Columba, trans. *The World of the Desert Fathers: Stories and Sayings from the Anonymous Stories of the Apophthegmata Patrum*. Oxford: SLG Press, 1986.

Waddell, Helen, trans. *The Desert Fathers*. London: Collins, 1936.

Ward, Benedicta, trans. *The Wisdom of the Desert Fathers: Systematic Sayings from the Anonymous Series of the Apophthegmata Patrum*. Oxford: SLG Press, 1986.

———. *The Sayings of the Desert Fathers: The Alphabetical Collection*. London: Mowbray, 1975.

———. *The Lives of the Desert Fathers*. London: Mowbray, 1981.

Wheeler, Eric P., trans. *Dorotheus of Gaza: Discourses and Sayings*. Cistercian Studies Series, no. 33. Kalamazoo, Mich.: Cistercian Publications, 1977.

# Related Reading

Chitty, Derwas James. *The Desert a City: An Introduction to the Study of Egyptian and Palestinian Monasticism under the Christian Empire*. Oxford, 1966. Reprint, Crestwood, N.Y.: St. Vladimir's Seminary Press, 1978.

Behr-Sigel, Elisabeth. *The Place of the Heart: An Introduction to Orthodox Spirituality*. Torrance, Calif., 1992.

Florovsky, Georges V. *The Byzantine Ascetical and Spiritual Fathers*. Belmont, Mass.: Nordland, 1987.

Holmes, Urban Tigner. *A History of Christian Spirituality*. New York: Seabury Press, 1980.

Jones, Chreslyn, Geoffrey Wainwright, and Edward Yarnold. *The Study of Spirituality*. Oxford and New York: Oxford University Press, 1986.

Lossky, Vladimir. *The Mystical Theology of the Eastern Church.* London: James Clarke, 1973.

Louth, Andrew. *The Origins of the Christian Mystical Tradition.* Oxford: Oxford University Press, 1981.

McGinn, Bernard, John Meyendorff, and Jean Leclercq. *Christian Spirituality: Origins to the Twelfth Century.* World Spirituality Series, vol. 16. New York: Crossroads, 1993.

McGuckin, John Anthony. "The Early Church Fathers" and "The Eastern Christian Tradition." In *The Story of Christian Spirituality,* edited by Gordon Mursell. Oxford: Lion Publications, 2001.

———. *Sages Standing in God's Holy Fire: The Byzantine Spiritual Tradition.* London: Darton, Longman, and Todd, 2001.

Printed in the United States
by Baker & Taylor Publisher Services